Path of the Sacred Pipe

D1559401

Path of the Sacred Pipe

JOURNEY OF LOVE, POWER, AND HEALING

Jay Cleve, PhD

QUEST

BOOKS

Theosophical Publishing House
Wheaton, Illinois • Chennai, India

Quest Books
Theosophical Publishing House
PO Box 270
Wheaton, IL 60187-0270

www.questbooks.net

Cover image courtesy Musee du Quai Branly/Scala/Art Resource, NY
Cover design by Drew Stevens
Typesetting by Wordstop Technologies, Pvt. Ltd.

Library of Congress Cataloging-in-Publication Data

Cleve, Jay.
Path of the sacred pipe : journey of love, power, and healing / Jay Cleve.
    p.   cm.
Includes bibliographical references and index.
ISBN 978-0-8356-0909-8
1. Calumets.   2. Indians of North America—Rites and ceremonies.
3. Indians of North America—Religion.   4. Vision quests.   5. Spiritual life.
I. Title.
E98.T6C45 2012
299.7—dc23   2012022950

Printed in the United States of America
5 4 3 2 1 * 12 13 14 15 16

To my teachers, Sun Bear and Wabun Wind.

TABLE OF CONTENTS

Acknowledgments

To Richard Smoley, editor, for his interest and confidence in the book; Sharron Dorr, publishing manager, for her orchestration of the book; Betsy Robinson for her careful and sensitive editing; Jessica Salasek for her enthusiastic publicist work; my wife, Susan, for her many searches and researches on the Net; and my stepson, Patrick Windmiller, for all the computer support.

Author's Note

Capitalization of special terms in this book is used to refer to something sacred, holy, or otherworldly.

When discussing pipes in general, I use the lowercase *p*; when it is a Sacred Pipe, specified as such, that has been gifted by a Spiritual Messenger or the Great Spirit, or has been blessed and awakened, I use an uppercase *P*.

When I use *heaven* or *heavens*, referring to the sky, I use a lowercase *h*; when I mean the spiritual realm, and not simply the blue sky, I capitalize. When referring to the physical sky above, I use a lowercase *s*, but the spiritual Sky is capitalized. Similarly, when I'm referring to the sacred planet, as an entity or being, I capitalize *Earth*; when I'm referring to the land, e.g., setting stones on the ground (earth), I don't. When I mention a direction on the compass, I don't capitalize. When I discuss the sacred Powers of the Cardinal Directions, I capitalize, i.e., *east* becomes *East*.

Similarly, when discussing real animals or birds on the earth plane, a lowercase letter is used, such as *e* in *eagle*. *Eagle* is capitalized when it represents the medicine archetype representing the power of Eagle. The same holds true for all of the power animals described in this book.

Introduction

Prophesied "Age of the Pipe"

The year is 500 AD, and Gray Wolf is standing on what is now called Bear Butte near Rapid City, South Dakota. He is facing east on a cold spring morning, holding his Sacred Pipe. As the rising sun turns the distant hills to pink, his aged hands place the last pinch of tobacco into the pipe bowl. After lighting the pipe and taking his first puff, he blows the sacred smoke to the heavens, to the Creator, and sends a puff to Mother Earth. He then blows smoke to each of the Four Directions. After holding the bowl with stem pointing to the sky and beseeching Grandfather and Grandmother Eagle to send his prayers to the Great Spirit, he slowly smokes, giving thanks and asking for health and healing for himself, his tribe, and the Earth.

It is 2012 AD on a chilly spring morning in Wisconsin, and I am standing on a cliff overlooking Devil's Lake. As I watch the first rays of sunlight paint the sky just above the frosted hills, I remember that it has been twenty-five years since I smoked my first pipe. In this timeless moment, I feel the presence of the grandfathers and grandmothers—the ancient ones, the keepers of the land. A thrill rushes up my spine as bits of ancient memories stir in the deeper recesses of my mind. And I realize, and sometimes even remember, that the ritual I am performing is older than the trees, even perhaps older than the hills.

Ancient memories? That the pipe ceremony is embedded in the collective unconscious of Americans was driven home to me a number of years ago when my stepdaughter asked me to do it during her wedding, before she and her fiancé took their marriage vows. As I took off my shoes and put a large, beaded medallion over my tuxedo in preparation for the ceremony, she felt some trepidation. How would 150 white, middle-class yuppies respond to an unusual ritual they probably knew nothing about? But as I began the ceremony—pointing the pipe stem to the heavens, blowing smoke to the above and below, turning, pointing the pipe stem and blowing smoke in each direction, and then beseeching the Eagle to send our prayers—I felt the crowd totally with me, sitting silently in rapt attention. Later, at the wedding reception, about a third of the group came up to one of my family members or to me and commented on the ceremony. Few of them had been to a pipe ceremony before but they were deeply moved, and a few said it felt "familiar." With tears in her eyes, one wedding guest said to me, "I have never been to a pipe ceremony, but I 'remember' it!"

The great psychoanalyst C. G. Jung said that when he treated Americans, he often found Native American symbolism and archetypes in their unconscious—even those who had no interest in Native culture or spirituality. And over the years I have spoken to many people on spiritual paths that didn't involve Native interests or practices; they were surprised to find at least one of their spirit guides to be Native American. Why not? Natives have lived on American soil for thousands of years and the ancient ones are part of the land, the very air we breathe.

Just how old is the pipe ceremony? There is recorded evidence that the ritual use of the Sacred Pipe dates back 600 to 1,500 years. But it actually goes back to ancient times. In the Americas, the parents of cultivated tobacco have existed for over 8,000 years. From the very beginning, tobacco may very well have been primarily for ritual, and the plant itself sanctified. Find the first pipe and one finds the first pipe ceremony. The use of the earliest tubular pipes dates back between 3,000 and 4,000 years.[1]

The Native American sacred ways, the Good Red Road,[2] and the ceremonies and practices have survived until today because they were protected over the centuries. But Jim Tree, Cherokee ceremonial leader and Keeper of the United Nations Turtle Pipe, points out that we aren't living in the same times and situations that warranted secrecy before. We are in a transitional time—a time when pipes are turning up all around the world—working toward a new way of being for humankind.[3]

Today, more and more Natives and non-Natives alike are being drawn to the Sacred Pipe. Some non-Natives are becoming pipe carriers: they obtain a pipe, receive training, and have their pipe blessed and awakened by a medicine man or woman.

The wise and powerful healer and spiritual chief of the Teton Sioux, Frank Fools Crow, puts the need to share Native teachings very strongly: "The power and ways are given to us to be passed on to others. To think or do anything else is pure selfishness. We only keep them and get more by giving them away, and if we do not give them away we lose them. . . . The survival of the world depends upon our sharing what we have and working together." He adds, "The ones who complain and talk the most about giving medicine secrets away are always those who know the least."[4]

THE TIME IS NOW

Ed McGaa (Eagle Man), a Lakota author, writes with some pride about the expansion of the "Rainbow Tribe," a worldwide "tribe" made of people from all colors and races.[5] Some of the greatest of the medicine people—Black Elk, Fools Crow, Rolling Thunder, and many others—were not only willing to share teachings but actually sought out non-Natives to teach. American scholar and author Joseph Epes Brown discovered that Black Elk was *expecting* him when Brown finally located the great medicine man. Hopi elders *asked* Frank Waters to write on Hopi philosophy and prophesy.

In 1989, a year after I began work with Sun Bear and had finished a lengthy paper on the Sacred Pipe, he encouraged me to keep writing and to tell Wabun Wind—his medicine helper, author, and coauthor—that I was a published author. After I wrote the pipe paper, Wabun had me present the teachings to the advanced pipe group.

Several years later, after receiving training from Sun Bear, Wabun Wind, and Shawnodese, empowering us to awake Sacred Pipes, Sun Bear conducted a ceremony bringing each of us in our small training group into his lineage—passed down through his uncles, both medicine men.

Over the twenty-five years I have been a pipe carrier, I learned that many of us who have no Native blood are "grabbed," at some point, by the pipe; the teachings have felt familiar; we "remembered" them. Many pipe carriers I have spoken with report that their teachers have told them they had many past lives as Native Americans. Some of these memories awaken even before they take up the pipe.

In 1998, a brief summary of the paper I wrote for the Bear Tribe was published in *Gnosis: Journal of Western Inner Traditions*.[6] After adding a few things to the paper, I set it aside—perhaps waiting for a Native American to write a book on the Sacred Pipe. Prior to 1990, the only book dedicated solely to the Sacred Pipe was *Offering Smoke* by Jerome Paper, a university religion professor.[7] The book was solid and scholarly but not one that invited readers to become personally involved with the Sacred Pipe.

At the age of seventy-one, toward the end of a large writing project, I suddenly felt compelled by a sense of urgency to write this book. But first I investigated whether others had written a book exclusively on the Sacred Pipe. To my surprise, I found only one slim volume: Jim Tree's *The Way of the Sacred Pipe*, published in 2004.[8] It is a very wise and respectful book, two-thirds inspiration (personal stories and experiences) and one-third practical information and advice regarding the care and use of the pipe. An excellent book, but a book was still needed to present in depth the history, background, and spiritual philosophy of the Sacred Pipe.

NATIVE PROPHECIES

There is an ancient prophecy that the time would come, after seven generations of subjugation by a white serpent that came from across the great eastern waters, when the children of the Earth from all Four Directions would come to the elders of the Native Americans to learn the ways of balance and harmony with themselves and the Earth.[9]

A later version of this prophecy was seen in a vision by Crazy Horse, the great chief and medicine man. He shared that vision with Sitting Bull during a ceremony with the Sacred Pipe:

> Upon suffering beyond suffering, the Red Nation shall rise again and it shall be a blessing for a sick world. A world filled with broken promises, selfishness and separations. A world longing for light again. I see a time of seven generations when all the colors of mankind will gather under the sacred Tree of Life and the whole Earth will become a circle again. In that day there will be those among the Lakota who will carry knowledge and understanding of the unity among all living things, and the young white ones will come to those of my people and ask for this wisdom. I salute the light within your eyes where the whole universe dwells. For when you are at that center within you and I am at that place within me, we shall be as one.[10]

Four days later Crazy Horse was murdered.

While living in California in the 1960s, I was told of an ancient prophecy: When whites began to dress like "Indians," it was time for the Native teachers to share their spirituality. I think the great medicine man Rolling Thunder spoke of it. And, in fact, in the '60s, hippies began wearing long hair, headbands, and beads. And for three to four decades we have seen this prophecy coming true all over the world.

As early as the 1980s and '90s, Sun Bear was teaching large groups of apprentices in Germany, where Native spirituality had caught fire. Jim Tree, Cherokee ceremonial leader and Keeper of the United Nations Turtle Pipe, reports that people from Australia continue coming to the United States to learn about the pipe. Tree says, "These Pipes are integral to ushering in the way of interdependence of all races . . . pipes are being dispersed throughout the world, their positive energies and efforts inter-lacing like a giant spider web covering the planet."[11]

Medicine Man Wallace Black Elk told me in the late 1980s about the prophecy that all peoples will again take up the pipe. He spoke of the Nation Pipe and said that this pipe is for all peoples. In his vision, he saw a circle of one hundred pipe carriers, and behind that another circle, and another—continuing on as countless circles of pipe carriers covered the Earth.[12]

Some time ago, Lakota medicine man John Fire Lame Deer declared: "We all must work together, both white and Indian, for we are all the children of the same Great Spirit."[13]

The Age of the Pipe

Despite the ancient origins of the Sacred Pipe, the pipe is coming into its own right now. We are now in the prophesized "Age of the Pipe" and the pipes are already spreading around the Earth. There is a feeling of a new era—the Sacred Pipe has returned to the people.[14]

Five hundred years ago in the Black Hills, White Buffalo Calf Maiden visited the Lakota, gifting them with her buffalo calf pipe. She vowed she would return in time of need, promising the people that the birth of a white female buffalo calf would be a sign of her return. She foretold that the sacred white female buffalo calf would change color four times. When White Buffalo Calf Maiden departed, she transformed into a white buffalo calf and rolled over four times. The first time, she turned into a black buffalo, the second brown, the third red, and finally white again. Bowing to the Four Directions, she took her leave. Soon after she left, herds of buffalo appeared to give their own lives so that the people might survive.[15]

Arval Looking Horse, born on the Cheyenne River Reservation in South Dakota, where he lives today, the Nineteenth Keeper of the Pipe gifted to his people by White Buffalo Calf Maiden, said that over the last hundred years his people weren't allowed to practice their religion and lost their way. A long time ago, he said that the birth of a white buffalo would mark the return to the old ways.[16]

And August 20, 1994, that in fact happened. David and Val Heider were there for the birth of a white, female buffalo calf on their farm in southern Wisconsin, near Janesville—about thirty-five miles from where I lived at the time. The calf, named Miracle, had brown eyes rather than the telltale pink nose and eyes of the albino.[17] A pure white, *female* buffalo that is not an albino is an extremely rare event—the chances of it happening are about one in six million.[18] Miracle was the first all-white, non-albino buffalo to be born since 1933, when a white *male* buffalo calf had been born.

Floyd Hand, a medicine man, traveled from South Dakota's Pine Ridge Reservation to Wisconsin after he had a vision about the white buffalo calf. Seeing a large obstruction in the bull's intestines, he predicted that that the calf's sire "would lay down his life for the calf." And just twelve days after the calf was born, the bull died. A vet's post-mortem revealed a large blood clot in the bull's stomach.[19]

David Heider said that two eagles had come around him when Miracle was being birthed. Medicine man Floyd Hand said that since his first visit, twenty-three eagles had come to the farm. Hand pointed out that the eagle is the messenger of the Great Spirit, and the eagles' appearances mean for humans to wake up.[20]

During her short life, Miracle turned four colors by the time she was six months old—white, black, red, and yellow—before she finally settled into a red and brown coloration as an adult. This is unusual for white buffalo calves, since all other white buffalo calves had remained white or whitish. But as the prophecy foretold, after turning the four colors, she would then blend with the herd until humankind came together, at which point she would once again turn white. But unexpectedly, at age ten, Miracle died of natural causes before she had a chance to turn white again. However, she had begun to lighten up again before her death.[21]

Native elders from all over the world see Miracle as the return of White Buffalo Calf Maiden. An early visitor to see Miracle was a dancer who performed concurrently with a major exhibit about the Aztecs at the Denver Museum of Natural History. He was supposedly Aztec and represented a quarter of a million Native people in Mexico. News of the white buffalo had already traveled through Mexico to the Indians of South America. They had all been waiting for this event.[22]

In the first two years after Miracle was born, seventy-five thousand people visited the Heider farm, coming from as far away as Russia, Australia, Japan, South Africa, and the Middle East—including the Dalai Lama, the spiritual leader of Tibetan Buddhism. Eventually, tens of thousands visited Miracle, seeing her as a symbol of hope and renewal and for harmony among all peoples, all races in our world today.[23]

Since Miracle's birth in 1994, a number of white buffalo calves have been born across the country—some were albino and many didn't survive. Others weren't pure buffalo, but a mix of buffalo and Charolais cattle or yak or other bovine. But as of 2006, there still remained a few legitimate white buffalo calves alive.[24]

However, that same year, a second white buffalo calf was born on the Heider farm, to live only three days. Then August 26, 2006, a white buffalo calf they named Second Chance was born to the Heiders. Birthed during a severe lightning storm, Second Chance, a white non-albino male, looked a great deal like Miracle. And like Miracle, the adult buffalo kept the new calf in the center of the herd, the most protected position, and the other mother buffalo stepped in to keep their own calves from being too rough with him.[25]

Three months after his birth, Second Chance, along with four other buffalo, was found dead under a lightning-struck tree.[26] With one-in-a-million odds that a buffalo calf will be born white, the Heiders have had three.[27]

Are the three buffalo part of the prophecy? In about 1996, a pure white buffalo—one of the four of the prophecy—was born on the Pine Ridge Reservation.[28] So with the Heiders' three, that made four—fulfilling the five-hundred-year-old prophecy portending that humankind was on the threshold of a thousand years of peace.[29]

Medicine man Floyd Hand pointed out that the message of White Buffalo Calf Maiden is for all people—not just for the Lakota and not just for the Indians.

John Tarnesse, Sun Dance Chief of the Eastern Shoshone tribe, born on the Wind River Reservation in Wyoming, said that when a buffalo is born white, the spiritual world sent it. Changing colors, the colors of all the peoples of the Earth, suggests that all colors of people are going to go back to their cultural roots because of the changes taking place in the white buffalo calf.

In the 1980s the Ojibwa medicine man Sun Bear said that if we trace our ancestry back far enough, we all have tribal roots. But many have lost touch with their indigenous roots and with Mother Earth.

People should go back to their own cultures because the calf is important for everyone, not just Natives, says Robert Pickering, author of a book on Miracle (*Seeing the White Buffalo*). "There is a resurgence of American Indian culture and spirituality. And perhaps on another level, the birth of the white buffalo signifies an awakening of spirituality in all peoples, a collective need to connect to the Earth and to seek deeper meaning."[30]

A New World Age

In 1977, at the request of Hopi elders, Frank Waters wrote a book about humankind moving into the New World Age[31] as prophesied by the Hopi. In more recent years, Sun Bear in 1992[32] and Tom Brown, Jr., in 2000,[33] among many others, prophesied upcoming earth changes.

Now as we transition in to the Age of Aquarius and move through 2012, ancient prophecies are creating a sense of urgency about the earth changes, earth cleansing, and the vital need for personal transformation. The earth is moving directly under the dark rift of the Milky Way, and we are transitioning into a New World Age predicted by not only the Mayans, Aztecs, Incas, Egyptians, and Chinese, but also the Native American elders from ancient times—especially the Hopi.[34]

The Maya were particularly interested in the period of time surrounding December 21, 2012, the time of the "galactic alignment," the time when the winter solstice sun aligns exactly with the position in the sky where the "ecliptic plane" (the sun's apparent path) intersects the galactic equator of the Milky Way, forming a "cosmic cross." This thirty-six–year process began in 1980—around the time Native medicine people increased sharing their teachings with non-Natives—and will end in 2016. From our perspective on earth, the December (2012) solstice sun moves across the galactic plane—an event that occurs every twenty-six thousand years—the result of which is attuning consciousness to higher frequencies.[35]

The prophet Nostradamus, in Europe in the Middle Ages, and the "Sleeping Prophet" Edgar Casey, in contemporary America, predicted cataclysms and cleansings occurring about this time. But, interestingly, Casey altered his predictions within a year or two of his prophecy: in 1933 he began to emphasize the importance of humankind's *response* to the earth changes. Even back then, he believed that the changes may not be as severe as predicted *if* people expand their consciousness to help with the transition.

There may be some scientific proof for this *participatory* consciousness: in September 2001, two geostationary operational environmental satellites—called GOES—orbiting the earth detected an immense rise in *global magnetism*.[36] At one point, the two satellites each registered a powerful spike of earth's magnetic-field strength. From a location of over twenty-two thousand miles above the equator, they detected the first surge, followed by an upward trend in the readings that topped out at nearly fifty units higher than any that had been typical for the same time previously. The time was 9:00 a.m. eastern standard time—fifteen minutes after the first plane hit the World Trade Center and about fifteen minutes before the second impact! Relooking at earlier data, the scientists discovered that the satellites recorded similar spikes during events of global focus in the past—such as the death of Princess Diana.

The factor that seems to connect the readings is clear: the *human heart*. Specifically, it is the heart-based emotion of the world's population that results from such events that seems to be influencing the magnetic fields of the earth.

The human heart generates the strongest magnetic field in the body, nearly five thousand times stronger than that of the brain. This field creates a doughnut-shaped pattern that extends well beyond the physical body and has been measured at distances of twelve to fifteen feet from the physical heart. Data suggest that this field may be so large that we may end up measuring it in miles—currently beyond the scope of the equipment.[37]

The heart's magnetic field responds to the quality of emotion that we create in our lives—positive or negative. Certain layers of earth's atmosphere, along with the earth itself, generate what is now being called a "symphony" of frequencies—some of which overlap with the ones created by the heart in its communication with the brain. It is this apparently ancient, and almost holistic, relationship between the human heart and the shields that makes life possible on earth.[38]

Scientists are discovering that strong collective human emotions have a measurable impact on the earth's geomagnetic field.

A new project called the Global Coherence Initiative, started by Princeton and one of its astrophysicists and cosponsored by a group called HeartMath, is involved in technological measurements of the heart. The goals of this initiative are to measure how earth's magnetic field affects human heart rhythms, brain activity, and emotions. Preliminary studies, such as those involving the GOES data, suggest that such effects are part of a *two-way relationship* between humankind and the earth's magnetic field.[39]

What is as significant as these discoveries is their timing: during the time of fear about earth changes, scientists have synchronistically discovered something humankind can *do* about them.

Introduction

Seers and sages, past and present, are predicting a time of a world shift and a need to move into a larger mind—transforming and raising consciousness to align with the radical shift, expansion, and evolution of earth energies. And how better to help ease and facilitate this transition than performing the Sacred Pipe ceremony? This ceremony, perhaps more than any other, helps humans connect with, bless, and heal the earth. The pipe ceremony is a *heart*-centered, *Mother Earth* honoring ritual to help heal the earth and humankind and to facilitate our transition into a New World Age.

1

The Sacred Pipe

Its History and Foundation

Legend has it that the pipe came from the Great Spirit, but how did humans receive it? Each tribe has its own myths and legends, and the story is often tied in with the creation of humans at the beginning.

In the Gros Ventres re-creation myth, the pipe was central to both the formation of the world and the release of the game animals. According to the Iowa Black Bear clan origin myth, the very first items received by the bears after they came out of the earth were a pipe bowl and then a pipe stem.[1]

The pipe was given to the ancestors of the Arapaho at the beginning of the world when the Turtle brought the earth up from under the water. The pipe was given to the tribe by the Duck, who, after the land appeared, was swimming on the top of the water.[2] The original pipe was given to the Blackfoot by Thunder, the spirit-person responsible for thunder and lightning.[3]

For the Cree, the Sacred Pipe was the parting gift from the Creator. Within the Cree creation myth, after the first man and woman were created, they were given the gift of the Pipe:

> "My children," Manitou said, "I am going far away. I am going up where nobody will see me. However, I am leaving you certain things—main things that are very important. There will be four of them: Fire, Pipe [bowl], Pipe stem, and sweetgrass.

"If, in the future, you wish to make any connection with me, these are the things to be used. And they must be used in this order: First, upward, in memory of your Creator; next, to the spirits of the Four Directions; and lastly, to Mother Earth."[4]

Hence, the Sacred Pipe is the first gift to the original couple from the spirit realm for a Plains Cree.[5]

CREATOR'S GIFT OF THE SACRED PIPE AT PIPESTONE

Among the many legends about how the first pipe came to humans, the following is one of the most common stories:

In centuries past, there was a battle raging around several tribes on the site where Natives from all over the country now come to quarry the red pipestone for their pipes. It is said that so many people were killed that the blood soaked deep into the ground and mixed with the earthly flesh of our Mother.

The Great Spirit saw the slaughter and was very sad that the people had forgotten how to live in peace with one other. He sent his messenger to stop the fighting. This powerful one appeared on the rock cliff overlooking the battle. He commanded the fighting to stop, and all obeyed—so powerful was his voice and command. He then scooped up the mixture of blood and earth and formed it into a Sacred Pipe bowl.

He made a stem out of the nearby hollow core branch of a sumac tree. He described to all present the meaning and medicine (power) of the red stone bowl and the wood stem. He commanded that, from then on, no decisions concerning war or other important things were to be made without the equal balance of both male and female input, and that requests for guidance concerning these issues be made to the Great Spirit through the Sacred Pipe.

He went on to teach many aspects of the Sacred Pipe: how it would transform prayers, first from a thought into physical form (through tobacco), and then through the transforming energy of fire into the spiritual form (smoke), drifting our requests up to the attention of the Great Spirit. He said that the Sacred Pipe acts as a kind of portal between the spiritual and physical worlds.

He then presented several Sacred Pipes to various spiritual beings who had come with the Great Messenger, assigning them to go to all the various nations on Turtle Island (North America) and instructing them in proper use of the pipes. He said that when a Sacred Pipe was awakened for the first time by smoking it, he would send a spirit helper to live in it to show the people the way of peace and harmony, both personally through an individual's Sacred Pipe, and corporately through the Ceremonial Pipe. The spirit's residence in the Sacred Pipe is one reason Natives never say false or boastful things in the presence of a Sacred Pipe, for it will reveal the truth of what is said.

These spiritual beings then went into the Four Directions and presented the Sacred Pipes to many nations, at places considered sacred to them. One of these places is a sacred lake in the Smoky Mountains, where a great serpent presented it to Red Arrow Woman of the Cherokee. Another is Bear Butte in South Dakota, where the White Buffalo Calf Maiden gave it to the Lakota Nation.

White Buffalo Calf Maiden's Gift to the Sioux

Nick Black Elk, a well-known medicine man, gives a beautiful account of the gifting of the Sacred Pipe to the Lakota by the White Buffalo Calf Maiden (which I've summarized):

Long ago, two scouts were looking for bison. When they came to the top of a high hill and looked north, they saw something coming from a distance. When it came closer, they cried, "It is a woman!" One of the scouts had bad thoughts, but the other said, "This is a sacred woman; throw all bad thoughts away." When she came closer, they saw that she was wearing a beautiful white buckskin dress, and her hair was very long and she was young and quite beautiful.

She knew their thoughts and in a voice like singing she said: "You do not know me, but if you want to do as you think, you may come." The foolish one went; but just as he stood before her, there was a white cloud that came and covered them. When the cloud cleared, the beautiful woman emerged, while the foolish man was a skeleton covered with worms.[6]

The sacred woman told the remaining scout to return to his people and tell his chief, Standing Hollow Horn, to prepare a large teepee, gather all his people, and make ready for her coming. When all were ready, the woman entered the lodge. Standing before the chief she held out a sacred bundle with both hands saying: "Behold this and always love it! It is *lela wakan* ("very sacred"), and you must treat it as such. No impure man should ever be allowed to see it, for within this bundle there is a Sacred Pipe. With this you will, during the winters to come, send your voice to Wakan Tanka, your Father and Grandfather."

Then she took from the bundle a pipe and a small round stone that she placed on the ground. Holding the pipe with its stem pointing to the Heavens she said: "With this Sacred Pipe you will walk upon the Earth; for the Earth is your Grandmother and Mother, and She is sacred. Every step that is taken upon Her should be a prayer. The bowl of this Pipe is of red stone; it is the Earth. Carved in the stone and facing the center is this buffalo calf who represents all the four-leggeds who live upon your Mother. The stem of the pipe is of wood, and this represents all that grows upon the Earth. And these twelve feathers that hang here where the stem fits into the bowl are from Wanbli Galeshka, the Spotted Eagle; and they represent the eagle and all the wingeds of the air. All these peoples, and all the things of the universe, are joined to you who smoke the pipe—all send their voices to Wakan Tanka, the Great Spirit. When you pray with this pipe, you pray for and with everything."

When the mysterious woman left the lodge she walked a short distance, looked back at the people, and sat down. When she arose, she had become a young red and brown buffalo calf. Then the calf walked farther, lay down, rolled on the ground, and became a black buffalo. The black buffalo walked farther, rolled on the ground, and became a brown buffalo, then red, and then returned to white. This buffalo walked farther, stopped, and after bowing to each of the four quarters of the universe, disappeared over the hill.[7]

Where did this White Buffalo Calf Maiden come from? Father William Stolzman, who was a member of the Rosebud Medicine Men and Pastors' Meeting group for several years, was present when the question was asked to a group of old medicine men. Apparently the story is very old and known by only a few.

A long time ago, a band of Lakota went down near Denver and were massacred; only a woman and her child escaped. It was a girl-child, still sucking at the breast. One day the woman was lying with her daughter nursing when, unexpectedly, she felt something shake her shoulder. She turned around and discovered that it was a starving buffalo calf. She took pity on it and let it suck beside her infant. The child and the calf grew up together. When the child became a maiden, the buffalo calf grew up to become the chief of all the buffalo, and he gave himself to the maiden in the form of the pipe. The maiden lived with the buffalo and traveled north with the herd in the summer, and that is where she came from.[8]

There are many descriptions of the various spiritual beings that brought the gift of the Sacred Pipe to the nations. But when it is a human being who brings the Sacred Pipe, it is almost always a woman.[9] Sun Bear, an Ojibwa medicine man, said that Day Break Star Woman brought the Sacred Pipe to the Ojibwa. He explains that she, Evening Star Woman, Red Arrow Woman, and Buffalo Calf Maiden are all the same person. But myths of Day Break Star Woman, for example, occur farther north, where there weren't buffalo.[10]

Chapter 1

THE SACRED PIPE IN NORTH AMERICA

Prior to the contemporary spread throughout Native cultures in sub-Arctic North America, the pipe had a range from the Rocky Mountains to the Atlantic and from the Gulf of Mexico to James Bay.[11] It didn't penetrate to the Pacific Coast, where tubular pipes continued in use, or the cultures of the Southwest, where tubular pipes ("cloudblowers") and elbow pipes with a short reed stem were used.[12] Unlike tubular pipes, most other pipes came in two pieces: bowl and stem.

Many of the early explorers and missionaries in the Americas noted the ritualistic use of the pipe. In 1535, Cartier observed the pipe being smoked along the St. Lawrence.[13] In 1607, Captain John Smith reported that the Werowance (chief) of the Rappahannock, a tribe of the Powhatan Confederacy, conducted elaborate pipe ceremonies. And in 1615, William Parker reported that the first thing the Powhatan did was offer their pipe.[14] In 1673, Father Marquette likened the pipe to the "Scepter of Kings" and the "Arbiter of Life and Death."[15]

Members of the Lewis and Clark expedition regularly saw rituals in which the pipe was used. In the nineteenth century, Jesuit priest Pierre-Jean De Smet also contributed extensive commentaries pertaining to Indian life and the pipe that presided at all feasts and ceremonies.[16]

In a 1939 address to students in Saskatoon, Dan Kennedy, an Ochan-kugahe, explained that the Native American understanding of the Sacred Pipe is like the "Ark of the Covenant" and the "Ten Commandments"—a symbol of the Great Spirit's Covenant with the Natives.[17]

Philosopher, poet, and anthropologist Hartley Burr Alexander explains: "No symbol native to the peoples of America has more profoundly stirred the imagination of the immigrant white race than that of the ceremonial pipe of the Indian—the hobowakan, the calumet, the pipe of peace . . . "[18]

There were many special reasons for smoking the pipe. It signaled the friendly reception of a stranger and afforded someone safe transport among other tribes. Smoking the pipe reflected the willingness to discuss an issue. Sometimes when someone did not seem to be telling the truth, the person was asked to smoke the pipe while talking—to test the person's willingness to be truthful or insure that the truth was being told.[19] Also, it was used as the formal act of acceptance of an agreement, much in the same way we use the signing and sealing of a contract.

Offering smoke (the pipe) was included in entering into peace negotiations. Early traders on the Upper Missouri River documented a ceremony called "trading on the pipe," placing pipes on the ground as "witnesses" to the fairness of the trading. Other times, a pipe was "sent around" to bands of a tribe to obtain individual or group participation in a raid or war party. Smoking a pipe "sent around" thus bound a man to accompany the party.

WHITE BUFFALO CALF MAIDEN'S PIPE TODAY

For years, the Cheyenne River Reservation of central South Dakota has been the place where the White Buffalo Calf Maiden Pipe has been kept. There are no markers that direct a traveler to the reservation's main town, a small, out-of-the-way community called Green Grass, twenty miles from Eagle Butte. Yet pipe carriers make a pilgrimage to Green Grass to "recharge" their pipes from the original pipe of the Sioux.[20]

Stanley Looking Horse passed on the caretaker duties of the Keeper of the Sacred Pipe to his son, Arval, the nineteenth caretaker. Arval said that just before a Keeper of the Sacred Pipe dies, he or she has a vision of whom to give the pipe. It's always given to a blood relative. In 1966, when Arval was twelve years old, his grandmother had a vision just before she died that the pipe should go to him. She taught him how to be the Keeper of the Pipe, and his father, Stanley, told him the rest later.[21]

Stanley Looking Horse says that the White Buffalo Calf Maiden brought the Sacred Pipe to the people near Devil's Tower. His son, Arval, says that he can trace the movements of the Sacred Pipe in stages to its current location. The Sioux first came to the Black Hills in 1775 to 1776, and by 1805 were in control of the territory.

Lakota medicine men call the original Sacred Pipe *Ptehincala Hu Cannupa* (Buffalo Calf Leg Pipe). Max Blacksmith, who grew up on the Cheyenne River Reservation, said that in the 1920s his father, John Blacksmith, told Max that he saw the original pipe at Green Grass and he said that it looked like a buffalo calf leg and its hoof.

Well-known medicine man John Fire Lame Deer said that he saw the Sacred Pipe in 1935. Lame Deer went to Green Grass and the old woman who was at the time Keeper of the Pipe was expecting him. When she opened the sacred bundle there were *two* pipes. She pointed out the older pipe, the *original* Sacred Pipe, which was about a foot long. Its stem was made from the left front leg bone of a buffalo calf and the bowl was made from some kind of anklebone. The bowl was strapped to the stem with a leather thong.

Lame Deer said that the *second* Sacred Pipe had a wooden stem about two feet long and looked much like the pipes used today. The woman told him that this was the *first* pipe, the one White Buffalo Calf Maiden instructed the chiefs to make.

Frank Fools Crow,[22] powerful Sioux medicine man and healer, said that he was taught and had seen in a vision that the original Sacred Pipe is much older than anthropologists believed. In the spring of 1976, Fools Crow went to Green Grass and was shown the pipe. He dated it to between 1200 and 1500 AD. (A holy man in the Black Hills told me it dated back to Columbus "discovering" America.)

The fact that the original Sacred Pipe is to be kept in the hands of the Keeper of the Pipe is clearly demonstrated by stories in which others take the pipe. For example, people once stole the original pipe from its keeper and were later killed. Lightning struck them dead and the pipe was mysteriously returned. Arval said that once the Indian agent sent the Indian police to bring the pipe to Cheyenne Agency, the reservation headquarters. As soon as they had the pipe there, Indian police began to die. The agent asked the keeper to come after the pipe.

He did, but instead of riding he walked all the way from Green Grass. By the time he arrived, all of the police involved in taking the pipe had died.[23]

In recent years, Father Paul Steinmetz, who spent many years on reservations, said: ". . . the Sacred Pipe is the key to understanding the original religions of North America from the Rockies to the Atlantic and from Hudson Bay to the Caribbean."[24]

And Father Michael Steltenkamp, a Jesuit priest who also spent many years on reservations, suggested that ". . . the pipe has become somewhat of a religious thread binding the many-patterned fabric of Indian culture and religion. . . . The Christian's breaking of bread is analogous to this centuries-old Indian practice. In both rituals, transcendence is perceived to operate and bind."[25]

THE SACRED PIPE TODAY

The bowl of the Sacred Pipe, called the *Chanupa* in Lakota, is the feminine aspect of a pipe. Pipes are carved out of many different kinds of stone: soapstone, greenstone, alabaster, red stone (catlinite), and black pipestone (steatite) from Canada and the United States. Alabaster makes an attractive pipe but tends to crumble from the heat of smoking.[26]

Very early in historic times, the Sioux (or Dakota) moved to the west and southwest. By about 1700, the Sioux were in control of the pipestone region, an area marbled with red stone, and they remained in control until the end of tribal days, about one and one-half centuries later. The red stone received its most widespread use during Sioux times, since the tribe's central focus is the Sacred Pipe.[27]

From early to modern times, many, if not most, Native American Sacred Pipes have been made of red stone from what is now *Pipestone National Monument* in southwestern Minnesota. But the proto-Mandan people who once frequented the area are not believed to have used the red stone—eventually named *catlinite* after George Catlin.

Catlin, who arrived in 1836, was a wanderer, writer, and artist who wrote about and drew pictures of Natives, their land, and their sacred objects. He was the first white man to describe what he called the "Red Pipe-Stone Quarry."[28]

When Catlin first arrived near this quarry, the Sioux were very angry with him, seeing him as an intruder, but he eventually managed to become accepted. Catlin explained that since the red stone was part of their flesh, it would have been sacrilegious for a white man to touch it or take it away. Catlin exclaimed, "A hole would be made in their flesh, and the blood could never be made to stop running."[29]

Catlin said that thirty-three years before he arrived, Lewis and Clark had passed Pipestone—"before the influence of traders had deranged the system and truth of things in these regions."[30] Catlin said that, in St. Louis, he often conversed with General Clark, who said that every tribe on the Missouri told him they had been to Pipestone, and that the Great Spirit kept the peace among his red children on this ground where they had smoked with their enemies.[31]

While near Pipestone, Catlin heard the story that long ago the Great Spirit called the Indian nations together. He stood on the red pipestone rock, reached over and broke a piece from its wall, and made a huge pipe by turning it in his hand. Then he smoked it over the Indians and explained that this stone was red, their flesh, and they must use it for their pipes of peace. It belonged to them all, and their war-club and scalping knife must not be raised on its ground. When the Great Spirit took the last puff of His Pipe, his head went into a great cloud, and the whole surface of the rock for several miles was melted and glazed. Then two great ovens opened beneath, and two women—guardian spirits of the place—entered them in a blaze of fire. People say that they hear them yet, answering to the invocations of the medicine men that consult them when they visit the sacred place.

Another story about an incident that was to have taken place at Pipestone involved a powwow with a number of tribal chiefs. They couldn't come to any agreements, and wars among them appeared to be inevitable.

Though the Peace Pipe was right there, none of the chiefs was willing to smoke it or even pass it around. But then a woman with a baby strapped to her back passed by the Peace Pipe. And as she walked by, the baby reached out and touched the pipe. Humbled, the chiefs began to look at the effects of their decisions in light of the next seven generations, and they then smoked the Peace Pipe together.

It's unclear when Natives began quarrying pipestone from the area. (The people at *Pipestone National Monument* say that there is evidence that quarrying occurred three thousand years ago.) Quarrying moderate quantities probably began between 1600 and 1650. It isn't known exactly how they did it. But today a layer of earth is shoveled away from the quartzite ledge. Then workers with sledges and crowbars—substitutes for the stones and long sticks of their ancestors—break and remove the quartzite from above the pipestone layer. This layer currently lies at a depth of eight to ten feet below the surface of the quartzite. Finally the pipestone layer is reached. It is over a foot thick but is divided into sheets by a soft, shaly deposit. These sheets are from one to three inches thick and are carefully removed for use in making pipes.[32]

To make a pipe, modern craftsmen first square up a block of stone with their saws and then cut easily, though slowly, with steel tools. They then scribe the outline of the pipe bowl on the stone, sometimes using a sheet metal template as a guide. The stone is then cut to rough shape with a saw. Primitive workers working freehand probably sawed the stone with thin flakes of flint.

Craftsmen do the rest of the shaping with woodworkers' rasps and with metal files. Successively finer files are used until a smooth surface is produced. Primitive workers used stone scrapers, blocks of quartzite or sandstone, or sand to smooth the surface of the stone.

Stem and bowl holes are then drilled carefully to avoid splitting the stone. Modern workers use brace and twist drills, but their ancestors probably used stone drill points and reamers. When metal became available through trade, knives, arrow points, and hoop iron scrapers were used to drill and ream these cavities. A final polish of beeswax is applied to the bowl when it is finished. Craftsmen's ancestors probably used various kinds of fat and tallow for this.

The Pipestone area owes much of its popularity to Catlin and to Henry Wadsworth Longfellow. But it took years of hard work, discussions with the government, governmental backsliding and passivity in the face of illegal quarrying, and even building at Pipestone by white people before the Department of the Interior recommended that certain boundary changes be made and that quarrying, rather than mineral, rights be reserved to Indians of all tribes. A bill to that effect passed the Senate in August 1937 and President Franklin D. Roosevelt made *Pipestone National Monument* a legal reality, a sacred area to be visited by all. Since 2000, yearly visitors to Pipestone number from sixty-three thousand to eighty-two thousand.

Under the supervision of the United States government and tribal authorities, the stone can be harvested only in the old, traditional way—and only by registered Native Americans. No power tools are used, and it is grueling work to break up the ten-by-fifteen-foot–thick layer of hard quartzite that covers the thin layer of pipestone below it. Today, many of those who remove the stone from the quarries give offerings back to Mother Earth before removing her "skin" to retrieve the precious layer of sacred stone. Some offer their own flesh.

STEM OF THE SACRED PIPE

Pipe stems, the male component of the pipe, were and are usually straight and made of wood—ash, sumac, or other types—selected for their soft, pithy core, which could be easily removed. Stems are still made by the traditional methods of burning out a core from sumac or splitting and hollowing ash or some other hard wood. Some stems are relatively thin and flat, others round. Some are quite plain, while others are decorated with braided porcupine quills, horsehair, feathers, totems, beadwork, hides, and other colorful materials that may represent one's personal helpers.

PIPE BAG

The pipe bag is very important, since it represents the body that houses the Sacred Pipe, which represents the heart of the body. In Lakota, the pipe bag is called the *Cantojuha* or "Container of the Heart." A pipe bag can be very elaborate with intricate beadwork or quillwork on it. The designs usually represent the medicine of the Sacred Pipe, such as the medicine of the Wolf, Buffalo, or Hawk. This is to acknowledge the responsibility one has to the pipe.[33]

TYPES OF PIPES

Though the Sacred Pipe was used widely throughout North America *and* was in use in South America, it is with the Plains Indians that the pipe had its most widespread use. In a booklet put out by the Pipestone Indian Shrine Association, *Pipes of the Plains,* we learn the many and varied pipes that were used down through the years.[34]

The most elementary pipe form is that of a tube. The Pueblo culture continues to maintain the ritual use of tubular pipes and also uses an elbow pipe with a short reed stem. The separate-stemmed pipe has not been adopted.[35]

Many of the tube pipes were made of bone, usually a section of the leg bone of an antelope, deer, bison, or other animal. Often these bone tubular pipes were reinforced by wrapping them with sinew, making the pipe less likely to crack when hot and easier to hold. Stone tubular pipes were also widely in use, and some of these are still in the possession of certain tribes—for example, the Cheyenne. Some are all stone and look like an enlarged cigar holder.

L-shaped stone bowl pipes with separate wood stems were popular over the Plains country in historic times. These elbow pipes were easier to smoke than the tube pipes. A T-shaped style called the Plains, or Sioux, was widely used throughout historic times. This style was similar to the elbow but had a projecting point jutting out ahead of the bowl, the bowl in the middle producing a T-shape (an inverted "T").

Early pipes of both the elbow and Plains styles sometimes had a ridge, or crest, running along the top of the bowl—sometimes representing the crest on the head of a bird. A rarer pipe style is the disk pipe, associated with the Iowa, Oto, Osage, and neighboring tribes. The bowl is characterized by the small bowl bore ("hole") surrounded by a large, flat-topped disk.

G. A. West classified nineteen varieties of North American Indian pipes. Of these, seventeen varieties occur in the Prairies and the East. Most of these varieties of pipes can be found around the Great Lakes— an area of relatively easy diffusion. The Calumet was the most important ceremonial pipe used. The word *Calumet* was supposedly derived from the Norman word *chalumeau*, a reed. Though the form of the Calumet differed in various areas, this pipe had almost universal use as the "Pipe of Peace."[36]

As with all things of the world, the pipes come with the aspects of both male and female energies/attributes. This is reflected by the style of some modern pipes that began to appear around the time of the Caucasian invasion of Native American lands.

The most common image of a Sacred Pipe is the T-style pipe of the Plains Peoples. It is generally accepted that a T-style pipe is a male pipe and an L-style (elbow) pipe female. If you put a T- and an L-shaped pipe together, they form the cross of the Four Directions of the Medicine Wheel.[37]

It is thought that the T-style pipes came into existence to signify the shift from the matriarchal social structure of the Native people to a male-dominated society. Although temporary, this shift to the patriarchal social structure was considered necessary by some Natives, because of the change in their lifestyle. Previously, tribes had taken a stand-and-defend approach to intrusion by other tribes. However, the invasion of the Europeans forced the Native peoples to adopt a much more nomadic lifestyle as they were driven farther and farther from their homelands.

A village had to be able to react immediately to threats from the white soldiers by fleeing their homes.[38]

The male, defensive time is finally over. Now the shift is toward honoring both the matriarchal and patriarchal, which was the original intent of the gift of the Sacred Pipe. When the L-style pipe was predominant, the society was more matriarchal. Then, as the society shifted to more patriarchal, the T-style became prominent.

Newer pipes shaped like a medicine wheel reflect the trend toward a society where both the matriarchal and the patriarchal are joined in interdependence—both equal, and both needed for leading the people into the changes ahead. Some of these pipes are shaped like a wheel with "spokes" crossing and joining the central bowl.

It is only when we attain a balance of both our female and male sides that we can be the fullest expression of whatever it is we have been called to do and be. This applies to us personally, as a people, as a nation, and as a race.[39]

Tobacco and Smoking Mixtures

For the Winnebago, as well as other Native people, communication with the spiritual powers (the function of tobacco) is the primary condition for life; it comes before food itself. In Cherokee myths, we find that tobacco is obtained or brought back to the people when they are dying without it.[40]

It is generally accepted among scholars that tobacco spread from South to North America, although it has been argued that the pipe spread in the reverse direction. The earliest evidence for horticulture in eastern North America, preserved squash seeds, dates to over three thousand years ago, corresponding to the earliest tubular pipes dated to between three thousand and four thousand years ago.[41]

The harsher tobacco species, *Nicotiana rustica*, was commonly mixed with other substances to improve the taste.[42] It was smoked by some groups in the Columbia Plateau area of Washington and Oregon. Other species of *Nicotiana*, both wild and cultivated, were used throughout the area north of Mexico.

The tobacco used by the Plains Tribes was obtained from a number of sources. Some sedentary tribes, such as the Arikara, Mandan, and Hidatsa, cultivated large amounts of tobacco, and other tribes traded for tobacco.[43]

In the pre-contact days (prior to the European invasion), tobacco was raised and traded under very strict procedures. In many of the tribal cultures of North America, there were special Tobacco Societies that were responsible for planting, growing, and harvesting the sacred herb. They cared for it in a sacred manner and the health of the tobacco field often reflected the very health of the community.[44]

Tobacco was usually mixed with some other material such as dried red willow bark, the underbark of dogwood, sumac leaves, pungent herbs, bearberry (sometimes used alone in northern areas), rose bushes, and leadplant in addition to the leaves and small stems of these plants. Bearberry leaf was probably the earliest smoking material used by the Ojibwa.

Tobacco was also mixed with the inner bark of certain trees of the genus *Cornus*, such as red osier, the leaves of one of the sumacs when they have turned red in autumn, and raspberry leaves. All these plants are associated with red, a color representing blood, the essence of life. The outer bark of Red Osier Dogwood is as named, red; sumac leaves turn brilliant red; bearberry has red berries, and the dried leaves are similar to the green of Native dried tobacco leaves.[45]

The mixture of tobacco and other materials is called *kinnikinnick* in the Algonquian language and *chan sha'sha* in the Siouan languages. In most languages, the term applied to the mixture meant "mixed" or "mixed by hand." The Algonquian word is variously applied to a smoking mixture as well as to individual elements.[46]

Other popular ingredients that are used are yarrow, dear's tongue, mint, dried flowers, and sage. Mullein, which isn't native to North

America, has been used ever since its introduction, to help mellow the harshness of many mixtures. Tobacco itself, much more harsh and bitter, was cultivated by many tribes but, due to its strength and scarcity, was seldom used alone.[47]

Originally the fruit of tobacco was much smaller and far more concentrated than it is now. The original tobacco was so strong it could kill—or at least make a person quite ill—if taken in the quantities used today. In traditional pipe mixtures, it was a very small component, compared to the other things used in the mix.[48]

Some Natives mix together seven herbs, representing the seven nations of the world: the stone nation, two-leggeds, four-leggeds, winged ones, swimmers, crawlers, and plant nations.[49] The number seven is a sacred number in virtually all world religions that came later.

Tobacco has many uses besides the pipe ceremony. It has strong healing properties, especially when used as an emetic or poultice. And when a Sacred Pipe is unavailable, we can take a pinch of tobacco and offer it to Father Sky, Mother Earth, and the Four Directions. If we carry a pouch of tobacco in our vehicle or on our person, we can stop when we are taking a walk or driving to appreciate beautiful scenery, a sunset, a waterfall, and we can offer tobacco in gratitude.

If we are taking something from the earth—leaves of a plant, birch trees for a sweat lodge, or a cottonwood tree for a sun dance—tobacco is offered before taking them. Herbalists trained in indigenous traditions often make an offering of tobacco before picking the plant. The medicine person collecting roots or plants may pray a pipe to help locate a plant or herb—and hopefully communicate with it—and then leave a tobacco offering before picking it or digging up the root.

On special occasions, before a sweat lodge, or during a vision quest, we can make "prayer ties." A prayer tie is made when a pinch of tobacco is placed in a small square of cloth (often felt, cotton, or wool), the end is tied off, and it is strung along a strand of cord with other prayer ties. The maker places a square of cloth, about two inches by two inches, in the palm of the hand, usually the left hand, and takes a pinch of tobacco with the right finger and thumb. Holding the pinch, one can offer it to Sky, Earth, and the Four Directions, calling in the powers. At times, the person can hold it up to the Great Spirit, speak the prayer into the tobacco, and perhaps blow on it—giving it one's breath—and then tie the end closed with a string or cord. Each tie is added with intent and strung along the cord.

Jim Tree describes a prayer tie as a "ghost" because of its shape. In his tradition, the string is wrapped around the "neck" of the ghost four times (for each of the Four Directions) and tied with only one pass through—a kind of half knot. The prayers and intents are then released into the universe for a response. Prayer ties are a physical representation of a spiritual intention, held out to the forces of the universe, to continually remind them of requests for prayer.[50]

2

The Medicine Wheel

The Heart of Native Spirit and Prayer

When pipe carriers begin the pipe ceremony, they offer tobacco to Father Sky, Mother Earth, and the Four Directions—the Four Powers, the Four Winds. As they offer the pinches of tobacco, the prayers come from the content of the Medicine Wheel. The Medicine Wheel is both an embodiment of Native spirituality and a tool in the use of the Sacred Pipe.

THE CIRCLE

To begin to understand the Medicine Wheel, we need to look at the universe as a Sacred Circle.

Natives believe the universe to be a vast circle—a huge Medicine Wheel—made up of numerous circles. Native peoples view all of reality as a circle. As the great medicine man Black Elk once said, everything an Indian does is in a circle, and that is because the power of the world always works in circles. Everything tries to be round. All our power came to us from the sacred hoop of the nation. The flowering tree was the living center of the hoop. The sky is round and the earth is round like a ball and so are all the stars. The wind, in its greatest power, whirls in circles. And birds make their nests in circles, for theirs is the same religion as ours. The sun comes forth and goes down in a circle. And the moon does the same, and both are round. Even the seasons form a great circle in their changing and always come back again to where they were. The life of a man is a circle from childhood to childhood; and so it is in everything where power moves. He said that teepees are round like the nests of birds, and these were always set in a circle, the nation's hoop, a nest of many nests, where the Great Spirit meant for us to hatch.[1]

When Native elders and sages tell us of their revelations and visions from the Creative Source, God is a circle of white light. The circle is the universal sum of all symbols, as white is the totality of all color. The most powerful and universally occurring symbol in nature, the circle, is the omnipresence of the Great Spirit existing in everything created, everywhere, at all times. It is Source manifested as symbol.[2]

The circle is the symbol of the Great Spirit; and the center of the Medicine Wheel is motionless, the eye of the Creator. It is where the Great Spirit resides and all directions, medicine, power, and perspectives are concentrated—from which existence flows, to which existence returns—each emanating from and returning to the center. The circle speaks to us of the nature of life. We can find neither the point of beginning nor the point of ending to the circle; life is unending, eternal.[3]

THE MEDICINE WHEEL

There were twenty thousand circles of stones in this country before the Europeans immigrated here. These wheels were ceremonial centers of culture, astronomical labs, and places where people would come to mark the times and changes in their lives, as well as the life on the earth. They were places to pray, meditate, contemplate, strengthen their connection with nature, and to come to realize a higher degree of understanding of themselves and their relationship with all of creation.[4]

The circle—the "wheel"—is embedded in nature. There are many Medicine Wheels. Not only the universe, our solar system, and the earth, but each family circle is a Medicine Wheel.[5]

The Medicine Wheel circle can become a vehicle for determining the balanced direction of the growth of consciousness. It can show the movement of one's realization and awareness and focal point for centering one's self; or it can facilitate the spiritual communion with the supernatural. The Medicine Wheel can be a tool, guide, anchor, symbol, vehicle, map, or circle of protection for sacred ceremonies.[6]

The Medicine Wheel itself is constructed with stones in a sacred ceremony and can be used alone as a structured way to pray—for example, by doing a Sacred Pipe while moving around the wheel or simply reflecting on the stones that comprise the wheel.

The Medicine Wheel is a kind of mandala containing the entire cosmos of the Native American—each stone being associated with the many manifestations of the Great Spirit: power animal, time of day, season, stage in the human life cycle, element, plant, color, human characteristic, and feature associated with the cosmos. The Medicine Wheel is a template for the dance of life, an unending spiral of interdependence.

Constructed in a sacred manner, the Medicine Wheel can itself become a springboard of power that will allow us to link up with all the energies of the universe; it is the sacred hoop of the nations. Besides the demarcation of sacred space, the stones also represent the members of the earth community, all of whom sit in common council. For the world to come back into balance and harmony, the nations must be healed, and all of creation must come into right relationship with the cosmos.

But the Medicine Wheel involves Mother Earth teachings. It helps us connect with the powers of creation, not by connecting with the stars, but rather by bringing us down to earth.[7] Yet the stones placed on the ground comprising the Medicine Wheel, which begin with the Creator stone, along with other stones representing Sky Father (Father Sun—the Earth's star—and Grandmother Moon, all aspects of the Creator) bring down and anchor the powers of the cosmos onto Mother Earth.

But in Native tradition, the Great Spirit isn't the patriarchal God of Judeo-Christian tradition; it is a creative-conceptive force combining feminine and masculine potentials in harmonious balance. The Sacred Mystery reveals itself as the Powers of the Four Directions; and these Four Powers provide the organizing principle of everything that exists in the cosmos.[8]

To gain self-awareness and enlightenment, we must be in harmony with the Powers of the Four Directions and the Source of all of life. The Medicine Wheel, which is symbolized by a cross within a circle, is a blueprint for a path to wholeness and a ceremonial tool for achieving balance; it is the basis for all Native teachings.[9]

Hyemeyohsts Storm likens the Medicine Wheel to a mirror in which everything is reflected—not only the entire universe that is *out there*, but also the universe that is *within us*. By praying and reflecting upon the meanings of the Medicine Wheel or doing a Sacred Pipe in a sacred manner, we take the powers of the Medicine Wheel into ourselves.[10] And with the Medicine Wheel inside us, we have our own inner council—all the power animals and plant and mineral spirits around and within the wheel—that we can call on for help and healing.

In the symbol of the Medicine Wheel, the Powers of the Four Directions are represented by the four cardinal points—that is, where the cross intersects the circle.[11] (See Figure 2.1.)

Natives view life as a continuous circle. Life, for them, mirrors the cycling of the seasons, the daily rising of the sun, the phases of the moon.[12] Life isn't seen as linear with a beginning and end, but as a never-ending spiral in a sun-wise fashion. And all things—humans, rocks, plants, animals—are interrelated. Separation is an illusion.[13] The Medicine Wheel is a cosmic symbol embodying the signs, meanings, and teachings of the Native peoples.

Loomis suggests that within the human race, the red race are the givers to the human world, the black race the holders, the white race the receivers, and the yellow race the determiners. In the center are the rainbow people, the people of mixed blood. Since all humans have red blood, black pupils, white bones, and yellow marrow, all humans could become the energy catalyzing other humans if they woke up and moved

Figure 2.1. Basic Medicine Wheel: Stones radiate from the central Creator stone to the Four Cardinal Directions.

from the place assigned to them by birth to another place on the circle, and eventually into the center.[14]

By reflecting on the Medicine Wheel and the meanings and characteristics of the stones making up the wheel and what they represent, pipe carriers can remember the rich, multiple meanings and teachings for each of the seven directions: above, below, and the Four Cardinal Directions, and the center that is now within themselves as they fill and smoke their Sacred Pipes.[15]

Indigenous peoples think of minerals, plants, and animals as having certain powers, so these totems are protection spirits. Ceremony is a way for us to center our energy and connect with these spirit powers that can help heal both humans and the earth.

In Europe, especially England, and sometimes in the United States, mysterious circles appear in the middle of fields. Perhaps these crop circles are telling us to return to the way of the Medicine Wheel.[16]

During a Medicine Wheel gathering in Michigan in the early 1990s, Wabun Wind, coauthor of Sun Bear's book on his vision of the Medicine Wheel, invited us to go out to the large Medicine Wheel that had been ceremoniously constructed earlier. A rope was placed around the perimeter of the circle, with openings at the four "gates" at the Four Directions. As instructed, I walked to the rope and reached in with both hands. Though I wasn't attuned to energy much in those days, I felt the air within the Medicine Wheel push my hands back, as if the wheel were a dome of powerful energy.

Medicine Wheels were typically constructed on existing power spots—energy vortexes. But Wabun explained that a Medicine Wheel constructed in a sacred manner creates its *own* vortex.

By reflecting on the Medicine Wheel, we learn the deeper meanings of the earth and creation. In this book we will partially construct the basic Medicine Wheel in order to see how the spiritual cosmos of the Native American is conceptualized and structured, and to gain a deeper appreciation for the prayers and invocations used in the pipe ceremony that are embodied by the Medicine Wheel.

In the construction of a Medicine Wheel, the stone representing the Creator is the first of twenty-nine stones placed on the earth. The Creator stone is the center of the wheel: always creating, without beginning or ending, always moving, always continuing. From this center radiates the energy that creates the rest of the wheel. Then the stones *surrounding* the Creator form the circle of the wheel and represent the foundation of all of life. In Sun Bear's vision (see fig. 2.2, page 39), slightly to the east of the Creator stone is the stone representing Mother Earth: the being who gives us our home and our lives. Continuing in a sun-wise (clockwise) direction from the Creator stone, slightly to the southeast is the stone honoring Father Sun, who warms and quickens our lives. Then comes the stone for Grandmother Moon, placed slightly southwest, who guides our dreams and visions.

In the tradition I was taught (see fig. 2.3, page 61), the anchor stones for the outer circle are the four stones honoring the Spirit Keepers of the Four Directions: Wabun, the great Eagle of the East; Shawnodese, the Coyote, in the South; Mudjekeewis, the Grizzly Bear, in the West; and Waboose, the White Buffalo, in the North. The Spirit Keeper stones divide the circle into the quadrants that set the boundaries for the twelve moons that divide the year.

Completing the Medicine Wheel are four Spirit Paths, each consisting of three stones radiating outward from the Creator to one of the four directional stones—the Spirit Keeper stones—representing qualities that take us from daily life into the sacred space of the Creator.

After receiving permission from Spirit to smoke the Sacred Pipe, the pipe carriers begin the ceremony by offering the first pinch of tobacco to Father Sky and Mother Earth—the two primary aspects of the Great Spirit, the Creator.

Creator

The Creator is the beginning of life and its ending, the Great Mystery within all things and around all things, the universal energy, that which many address as God. In Native languages, the word for Creator is a verb, indicating the movement, activity, motion, pulsation of this sacred, never-ending force. The Creator stone teaches us about our own ability to create, our faith, our own sacredness, and our ability to develop to our fullest.

Earth Mother

The Earth Mother stone represents the love and new beginnings the Earth Mother always gives her children. The totems associated with this stone are clay in the mineral kingdom; corn, beans, and squash in the plant kingdom; and the great tortoise in the animal kingdom. It's the place in the Medicine Wheel that teaches about nurturing female energy within us and about the Earth Mother herself.

Father Sun

Father Sun stone represents the growth and clarity the sun brings to Earth Mother. Since ancient times the sun has represented the Creator. The sun gives abundant warmth freely, asking for nothing in return. The totems associated with Father Sun are the geode, the sunflower, and the lizard. This stone teaches about the core masculine energy and about the active principle of the universe. This is the place to go if we need more energy, if we need warmth and expansion. The stone also teaches about discrimination: the healthy ability to set limits, to say no when we need to. The sky is the direction of freedom and limitless possibility.[17]

Grandmother Moon

The next stone represents Grandmother Moon, honoring the trust that comes from the introspective energies of the moon. In many Native traditions the moon is considered the leader of feminine life, in part because women, like the moon, experience different phases and cycles.

Grandmother Moon teaches about a different aspect of feminine life than the Earth Mother does. This aspect of the feminine is the one strong enough to be receptive, courageous enough to surrender to life, wild enough to seduce the active forces, and visionary enough to conceive of new life coming from the old. Grandmother Moon dreams the children that Earth Mother nurtures.

The totems associated with Grandmother Moon are moonstone, mugwort, and the loon. This stone position on the wheel can help us with our dreams and visions. Grandmother Moon can aid us in increasing our intuitive and psychic abilities. And we can learn about our own sensuality as well as sexuality. We can explore the emotional side of our being and the parts of us that defy logic.

This is the stone to seek when we find ourselves fearing our own deepest emotions or when we need help understanding them. Grandmother Moon's soft, gentle light allows us to examine the shadow side of ourselves, the parts of ourselves buried so deep we fear looking at them in the full light of day.

Father Sun and Grandmother Moon are two aspects of Father Sky— all representing the Creator.

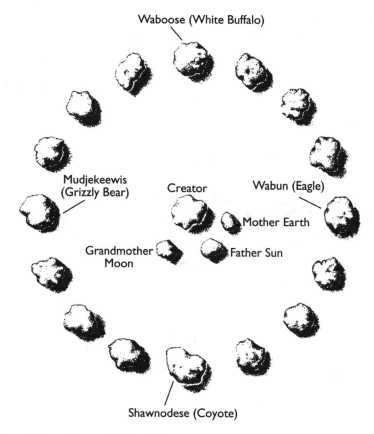

Figure 2.2. Medicine Wheel with the power animals of the Four Directions and the central Creator stone with the three stones representing the Creator.

Chapter 2

Spirit Keepers of the Four Directions

Once pipe carriers have invited in Father Sky and Earth Mother, they invite in the Spirit Keepers of the Four Directions by offering a pinch of tobacco to each of the cardinal directions before putting it in the Sacred Pipe.

Natives believe that animals were created first in order to be our teachers. In the creation myths of the Plains Indians, which are amazingly similar to the Egyptian creation story and biblical *Genesis*, the animals were created before human beings, so that in coming first and in their divine origin, they have a certain proximity to the Great Spirit—thus demanding our respect and veneration. In animals, the Native person sees actual reflections of the qualities of the Great Spirit; seeing animals serves the same function as revealed scriptures.

Animals are not lower or inferior to us. Because they were here first and are entitled to the respect always due to age in Native cultures, the animal beings are looked to as guides of human beings—indeed, in a sense, as our superiors. Thus, animals can be intermediaries or links between humans and the Great Spirit. This not only explains why spiritual devotions may be directed to the deity *through* animals, but it's also why contact with, or from, the Great Spirit comes to the Native American almost exclusively through visions involving animal or other natural forms.[18]

Though traditions differ, the eagle, coyote, bear, and buffalo often represent the Four Directions. These Spirit Keepers are powerful animals that reflect the basic virtues of the Creator.[19]

Eagle
Tobacco is usually offered first to the East, represented by Eagle, the chief over all winged creatures.

Many eagles mate for life.[20] The mating dance of the bald eagle is a breathtaking aerial display in which the two birds dip and dive in flight.

They then clasp each other's feet and plummet spinning to earth, mating, and then doing it again.

The male collects material and the female is the architect of the nest. Though a predator, the eagle helps the balance in nature by hunting only the weak and sick—helping to keep the world healthy by preventing the spread of disease.

Eagles are very efficient hunters and don't have to spend much time feeding themselves, Thus, they spend much of their lives experiencing the joy of flight, which reflects freedom, independence, and untamed energy. Perhaps this unfettered joy of living is why the eagle is such a long-lived bird and why rejuvenation, renewal, and longevity are also considered to be Eagle medicine.

Since time immemorial, Eagle has been revered by many different peoples for its medicine power. Several mounds with an eagle's image carved at the apex have been located in southern Wisconsin; they date back to 2000 BC.

Eagle is representative of and messenger to the sun, and humankind's connection to the divine. The eagle flies higher than any other bird, teaching us to live in the realm of spirit, yet remaining connected and balanced within the realm of the earth.

Eagle teaches us to broaden our sense of self beyond the horizon of what is presently visible. And it teaches us to overcome and ultimately conquer the boundaries of this world, helping us cross into other realms. Eagle is known for its ability to help us in developing shamanic powers—among them, soul travel or spirit journeying to alternate worlds. Invoking Eagle fills us with the ability to soar to great spiritual heights.

With Eagle's eyes, we can see with the Sunlight Vision, whose brilliant light sharply illuminates the truth against the murky backdrop of illusion. The clear vision enables us to see far, to view our own lives from a new perspective: to fly far above our mundane cares and worries, focusing on that which is most important—developing our spirits. We evoke Eagle for clear vision, illumination, and transcendence. Flying high, close to spirit, it is at this elevated angle that Eagle becomes detached from the earth and material things.

Eagle medicine is symbolic of honesty and correct principles, assisting us in perceiving the deepest truth at the heart of a given situation. Eagle facilitates communication with the divine for creative inspiration and vision. Eagle comes when it is time for us to connect with our higher self and divine guidance.

Eagle is connected with the east wind and the direction of spring, dawn, and rebirth, bringing messages of renewed life. If we are going through hard times, Eagle not only signals a new beginning, but also endows us with the stamina and resilience to endure the difficulties, providing us with a fighting spirit.

Eagle brings freedom from inhibition and gives us the ability to look ahead. Eagle lifts us up to the sunlight and speaks of opportunity to awaken both inner and outer visions, and it bestows the freedom and courage to pursue the opportunities.

Eagle represents a stage of grace achieved through hard work, understanding, and a completion of the tests of initiation that result in taking our personal power. It is only through the trial of experiencing the lows in life as well as the highs, and through the trial of trusting our connection with the Creator, that the right to use the essence of Eagle medicine is earned.

As we learn to fiercely attack our personal fear of the unknown, the wings of our soul will be supported by the ever-present breezes that are the breath of the Great Spirit.

Eagle represents the element of air, which is on the mental plane and is associated with the higher mind. It represents swiftness, strength, courage, wisdom, keen sight, and the ability to see the overall pattern of life, connecting with powerful spiritual beings and creating a stronger connection with spirit guides and teachers.

Coyote

The Spirit Keeper of the South is the wily, adaptable Coyote—the creator, teacher, and keeper of magic.

The coyote is born in the desert, yet takes a stark landscape and transforms it through its will to survive. Most predators of the world diminish, and yet the coyote endures. A coyote is less than four feet long and weighs about thirty pounds but can run for short distances at a speed up to forty-five miles an hour.

The coyote has learned to adapt itself to human civilization, frequently living within the outer boundaries of cities and towns. It is quite intelligent: sometimes a female will deliberately lure a domesticated dog out of familiar surrounds in order to kill it for food. Though often seen as a pest, coyotes have managed to extend their range because they have used keen intelligence and adaptive ability.

Unlike the wolf, the coyote isn't a pack animal, but stays in small family groupings of parents and offspring. Where the ecological balance has remained undisturbed, the coyote is the true scavenger who finishes off the remains of a kill. The coyote is more adaptable to the advancement of civilization than the wolf. But, like the wolf, coyotes are extremely loyal and their families exhibit similar social structure, posturing and communicating as their larger cousins do. The coyote has a very close-knit family unit and sometimes mates for life.

The father is very conscientious and participates in the care and rearing of the young. Both parents train their young in hunting techniques. The male cares for the mate while she is pregnant, helping to protect and feed her. If something happens to the mother, the male takes over the care of the young.

Coyotes do what they need to do to survive. For example, although coyotes prefer to live only with their mates, if hunting conditions are difficult, they will form a pack with other coyotes so they can all hunt more efficiently. Coyotes have even been known to form hunting alliances with badgers when it benefits them.

Chapter 2

Coyotes hunt from dusk to dawn in order to avoid hunters. They will often use cooperative hunting techniques and have a well-organized system of running down smaller prey. The chase occurs in relays, so when one coyote rests, another gives chase. This kind of cooperation hints at the energies that coyote can bring to our lives—an ability to stimulate cooperation to accomplish important tasks in the most efficient manner.

Among the coyote, even the adult is playful, sometimes chasing its own tail and rolling down a ravine as a result, or pouncing on a particular spot over and over again despite the fact that there's nothing there.

Coyote energies, tied to simplicity and trust, stimulate and renew innocence and awaken childlike wisdom, wonder, and humor.

Coyote likes to sing and enjoy a night chorus. Coyote is playful and fun-loving. Though Coyote has many skills, he looks for ways to do things that will not involve the use of his skills—through shortcuts. Coyote reminds us not to take ourselves or our lives too seriously, reflects the balance of wisdom and folly, and is often the wise fool.

Coyote is the archetypal Trickster, a mischievous jester whose constant pranks are his way of affirming and celebrating life. The Lakota call a medicine man with Coyote energy a *Heyoka*, which means "contrary" or "backwards-doing." The medicine man with Heyoka medicine keeps people off balance, teaching them by going in the back door, setting up the unfamiliar and unexpected.

But the reverence afforded Coyote should be tempered with caution, because Coyote isn't above playing a trick or two on those who invoke him. Mischief is, by nature, difficult to control, and there is no telling what Coyote will do. His tricks often get him into trouble, but in the end Coyote seems to always land on his feet. So we can invoke Coyote medicine when times are hard and we are having trouble seeing the way out of our problems; the ability to develop alternatives is one of Coyote's many medicine powers.

Coyote howls at the moon, chuckles at the sun, and his dry desert home blooms with the joy of life in his heart. Coyote plays the buffoon in order for others to learn and listen. Coyote maintains a sacred irreverence and plays the sacred clown, helping us cut through people who are phony, stuffy, deceitful, or take themselves too seriously. Sometimes it is the Coyote in us that makes us want to liven up a party or poke fun at someone who is too arrogant or stuffy or taking him- or herself too seriously.

Coyote people with an irreverent attitude, a penchant for mischief, and a willingness to question authority are given a special kind of protection from Coyote. Coyote isn't very good at keeping these people out of trouble because he isn't all that good at keeping himself out of trouble. But he can be called upon for getting them out of it once they have gotten into it—though he often waits until after he has extorted his measure of enjoyment at their predicament.

Coyote's sacred irreverence allows him to know that the authority we ascribe to many hierarchies is often unearned and misplaced. The bogus guru, phony expert, lying politician, and false prophet are all hilariously obvious to Coyote. We can call upon Coyote to help us see through the self-proclaimed "experts" who want us to pay them for the wisdom that is already ours.

Coyote is a spirit of the night, with great magical powers. And Coyote is the great changer, changing something from one thing to another, or changing itself into something else—creatively teaching us by keeping us off balance and surprising us.

Coyote medicine is the power of an irrepressible optimism that makes it possible to turn the bleakest circumstances into a winning situation. Coyote shows us the humor, adventure, and paradoxes in life and teaches us to laugh at the world and ourselves.

Coyote is a survivor and his medicine power, life-affirming. And Coyote exhibits cunning, stealth, opportunity, truth, and creativity.

Bear

The Spirit Keeper of the West, the grizzly bear, has been feared and revered since ancient times. Neanderthal people honored him by placing bear skulls on their altars. The bear has stirred imagination so much that even constellations were named for it—Ursa Major, the Great Bear, and Ursa Minor, the Little Bear. The seven stars of the constellation make up the Big Dipper. Bear has lunar symbology as well, giving it ties to the subconscious and even the unconscious mind.

The grizzly is looked upon with awe and warriors seek after it as a symbol of strength and courage. Bear is brave but also unruly and wild—human yet divine. But Bear medicine involves not only strength and protection, but also gentleness and love. Because of Bear's ability to walk upright, its soul is thought to be special, knowing all things, wisdom, and medicine.

Bear medicine is used for connecting with the secret rhythms of the earth. It is invoked when incubating ideas, plans, and dreams and bringing them to fruition. Bear helps us tap into the creative powers of our unconscious and teaches us how to cultivate groundedness and power, including the power of introspection. Bear is the sacred dreamer, seeker of truth, and teaches balance between activity and rest.

The brown bear is a creature of the moon. As prime matter, it speaks of returning to the primitive and imbues us with a strong instinct for survival. If we're working with the unconscious, we can invoke Bear for protection. Bear can act as a guide in the murky world of the subconscious.

Bear teaches us to go within (through hibernating) when we have problems, to seek knowledge through meditation, and to search for hidden wisdom in our dreams. Serene contemplation, quiet introspection, and calm meditation are Bear's wise medicine gifts.

The depth of a bear's sleep depends greatly upon the amount of stored fat. This reflects Bear's ability to teach us how to go within to find the resources needed for survival. During winter, a bear's kidneys shut down completely. Metaphysically, the kidneys are symbols of discernment and discrimination.

In winter, a bear enters the womb-cave to hibernate, to digest. It is said that goals reside in the West, and to accomplish the goals and dreams we carry, we must learn the art of introspection. To become like Bear and enter the safety of the womb-cave, we must attune ourselves to the energies of the Earth Mother and receive nourishment from the placenta of the Great Mystery, where all solutions and answers live in harmony with the questions that fill our realities. Bear helps us quiet our mind so that we can enter the silence and know.

Many tribes have called this space of inner knowing the Dream Lodge, where the death of the illusion of physical reality overlays the expansiveness of eternity. It's in the Dream Lodge that our ancestors sit in council to advise us regarding alternative paths that lead to our goals. The female receptive energy that for centuries has allowed visionaries, mystics, and shamans to prophesy is contained in the power of Bear medicine.

Bear is in the West, the intuitive side—the right brain. To hibernate, Bear travels to the cave, which is the center of the four lobes of the brain where the pineal gland resides. In the cave, Bear seeks answers while it is dreaming or in hibernation. For eons, seekers of the Dreamtime and of visions have walked the path of silence, calming the inner chatter, reaching the place of rites of passage, the channel or pineal gland.

Bear's ability to reemerge from sleep in the spring to take up the joy of life once again symbolizes death, rebirth, and renewal. Bear also reflects stamina, patience, defense, wisdom, intuition, listening, and the need to appreciate quiet within.

The bear is also associated with the medicine of herbs and roots. Bears dig up acorns, juneberries, and cherries—three ingredients frequently compounded with other herbs in making medicine. Bears are attracted to the herb osha and respond to it as a kind of ursine catnip. Bears roll on it and cover themselves with its scent. Males have been known to dig up roots and offer them to females as part of courting. When a bear comes newly out of hibernation, it eats osha if it can find it to cleanse its digestive system. Bears chew the root into a watery paste and then spit it on their paws and wash their faces with the herb and spray the herb over their bodies. Osha possesses strong action against bodily parasites.

Buffalo

The Spirit Keeper of the North is the buffalo; in America it is actually the bison. The bison is the largest terrestrial mammal in both Europe and America. With the extinction of the woolly mammoth, the bison was left as the largest herd animal in the Americas for the next ten thousand years.

The buffalo, representing the sacred life and abundance, was the very soul of the Native American, who derived food, clothing, and myriad other uses from the buffalo. Buffalo gave its hide to our ancestors to provide them with shelter. From the buffalo came meat and marrow, tongue, intestines, liver, other organ meats, blood, dried jerky, and fat for food. The tanned hide was used for teepees, moccasins, leggings, dresses, breechcloth, robes, bedding, belts, caps, mittens, bags, pouches, and dolls. Rawhide was used for containers, sheaths, shields, rattles, drums saddles, bridle and tack, ropes, masks, bindings, snowshoes, and ornaments. Horns were used for cookware, flasks, headdresses; the bone for knives, arrowheads, digging implements, sleds, war clubs, ceremonial objects, tools, utensils. Hair was used for headdresses, padding, stuffing, ropes, alters, and to string and tie ornamentation. The tail was used for ceremonial objects, whips, medicine switches. The bladder, paunch, and stomach were used for cooking vessels, water carriers, basins, buckets, and cups, toys, and ceremonial balls. Sinews were used for thread, bow-strings, binding, and bow backings. The brain was used for hide tanning, and the "chips" were used for fuel for the fire and incense for ceremonies.

Thus the buffalo became the manifestation of the divine for the Plains tribes. Its arrival always signaled abundance, as it does today. And the appearance of the buffalo often initiated a period of prosperity.

The American decimation of the Plains herds is notorious, a strategy devised to subdue the tribes through starvation. Even after the bison retreated from the woodlands of the east to the Great Plains, it was esti-mated that the herds numbered over seventy million. By 1900 there were fewer than one thousand buffalo left in the wild. White men killed more than sixty to seventy million buffalo, often shooting them from a moving train for sport.

Because of its desire to give the gifts that its body provided and because of its willingness to be used on earth for the highest good before entering the hunting ground of Spirit, Buffalo did not readily stampede or run from hunters—but often gave freely of itself.

The buffalo figures in many Native ceremonies. Most tribes had buffalo dance societies. The Cheyenne believed that if they placed horns on their headdresses they became bulletproof.

According to prophecy, the birth of four white calves heralds the beginning of a new age of prosperity for the Native American. Part of what White Buffalo Calf Maiden taught the Lakota is that they did not have to struggle to survive if right action was joined with the right prayer. If they united the mundane and the divine appropriately, all that would be needed would be available to them.

The hump at the buffalo's shoulder level implies that we must incorporate our efforts. Shoulders are symbols of the ability to embrace and hold life. Upon shoulders are carried either our burdens or our rewards. And the massive buffalo head implies the need to combine our efforts with the divine. The head is the upper region, a symbol of the heavens and the divine, the higher faculties. Both the mundane and the spiritual are necessary for manifesting what we seek.

The buffalo usually follows the easiest path, and when we join right action with the right prayers, the path for us is not difficult. The path opens up and flows easily, and we don't have to bull our way through things. We can pay attention to the synchronicities and flow with the natural rhythm of life.

Buffalo medicine is a sign that we can achieve nothing without the aid of the Great Spirit, and we must be humble enough to ask for assistance and then be grateful for what we receive.

When a buffalo was killed, every part of the buffalo was used. The buffalo gives itself completely. Great Spirit is prepared to meet our needs. But the buffalo also taught us to reciprocate and learn to give our all.

The spirit of the buffalo remains in everything. Even dried buffalo chips were treated with reverence and respect. When they were laid on a fire, their smoke carried prayers to the Spirit Buffalo. The holy man would blow smoke from his Sacred Pipe into the nostrils of a buffalo skull and then stuff them with sage so the prayer would remain inside the head to be heard by the Great Spirit. The buffalo represents gratitude, prayer, abundance, fertility, growth, and praise for all that is received.

Bison has female and male attributes. As bull, bison symbolizes warrior power. (Buffalo parts can be used for weapons.) In the Hidatsa creation myth, male bison produced tobacco for the pipe. The female aspect of the bison provided the peoples of the Plains most of what they needed for life.

Bear represents knowledge and exploitation of underground earth forces (roots and herbs), but in a strongly masculine manner. Buffalo represents the nourishing and life-giving force of the earth in a manner that expresses the principle of ideal womanly virtue.

Animal Ranking. There is a certain ranking of the animals, or of their underlying "spirit-power." Buffalo is the chief of all the animals on the surface of the earth and represents the Earth, the totality of all that is. It is the feminine creating Earth principle, the nurturing and life-giving forces that give rise to all living things. Grizzly Bear is understood to be chief of these underground earth forces and represents knowledge and use of these forces (roots and herbs) in a strongly masculine manner. And Eagle is the chief of the air, having supremacy over all the flying beings.

Other Spirit Keepers

The Eagle, Coyote, Bear, and Buffalo are honored most frequently as the Keepers of the Four Directions. However, every tradition is different, and other totem animals have been relegated to the directions in some tribes. The most frequently chosen are the Hawk, Wolf, and Cougar.

Hawk. Hawk is sometimes chosen as a Spirit Keeper of the East. The female is always larger, having much to do with guarding the nest. But both female and male care for their young and cling to their home territory for years. Many hawks mate for life, the Red-tail for example.

The hawk has vision eight times greater than humans, and though it can't fly as high as the eagle, it can maneuver better, hover, and stay suspended in the air longer than the eagle. Hawk has great endurance, yet balances between soaring, perching, and looking.

The Red-tailed Hawk has the ability to soar and glide upon the currents. Yet it's most seen perched patiently on treetops and utility posts, using its phenomenal eyesight to locate prey. It teaches us how to fly to great heights yet still keep our feet on the ground and be patient.

Hawk is one of the most intriguing and mystical of the birds of prey. It is the messenger, protector, and visionary of the air. The Lakota say that Eagle better carries messages to the Creator, whereas Hawk conveys tidings to and from the grandfathers and grandmothers of the tribe and is most associated with the Good Red Road. Ancient Christians saw Hawk as a symbol for resurrection.

Hawk is one of the most important messengers, being the greatest of the flyers. Just as Hawk can travel from Earth to Heaven to relay invocations and prayers to the earthbound, so can it bring guidance and comfort back from the Heavens. We can call upon Hawk medicine for the power to temporarily flee the confines of the earth plane when the burdens of this life threaten to smother our soul. Hawk floats far above the surface of a hunting ground bustling with life, but also with illusion. Hawk helps us keep perspective, see clearly, and choose carefully.

Hawk awakens our vision and inspires us to a creative life purpose. Hawk medicine can imbue us with the power to overcome a currently stressful or difficult situation. The test is our ability to observe the nuances of power lurking nearby. Hawk helps us become aware of signals in our life and teaches us to grab an opportunity that may be coming our way. Or Hawk may be bringing us the message that we should circle over our life, seeking a higher vantage point, to discern the hazards that bar us from freedom of flight.

The feathering of the Red-tail actually has two phases—lighter during the summer and darker in winter. The lighter color is often symbolic of more joyful and sociable kinds of energy, and the darker reflects a time to be alone or to withdraw a little. The Red-tail and its color phases help us guard against blazing so brightly and intensely we get burnout.

The red tail is very symbolic, being associated with kundalini, the seat of the primal life force. In humans, it's associated with the first chakra, located at the base of the spine. It teaches psychic vision and astral projection and is tied to the archetypal forces that teach beauty and harmony in moderation.

Rising to a higher level can bring a rapid development of the psychic energies. The Red-tailed Hawk helps us in balancing and using those senses appropriately and teaches the balance necessary to discover our true purpose in life. Hawk is a catalyst—to being open to the new, and stimulating hope and fresh ideas.

To the Pueblo, the Red-tailed Hawk is known as "red eagle."

Many tribes use hawk feathers in healing ceremonies and for bringing the rains and waters necessary for life.

Hawk is a great hunter, searching for knowledge and wisdom.

Hawk brings us the gift of deliberation, foresight, and the spirit of prophecy.

Wolf. In some traditions, Wolf is the Spirit Keeper of the South. Interestingly, despite many beliefs to the contrary, there has never have been a confirmed attack and killing of a human by a healthy wolf in the United States. In northern Wisconsin, wolves have been introduced directly into a whole new environment by rangers, and some of their behaviors have been influenced by human intervention—putting them into areas that have not had many wolves in the past. Competition among wolf packs is not natural in the wild; there, wolves tend to identify a territory and even limit the number of pups if the territory doesn't supply enough food. But human intervention can affect wolf behavior.

Wolves are the epitome of the wild spirit; they are the true spirit of the primal and unspoiled wilderness. Yet among themselves, wolves are friendly, social, and highly intelligent. Their sense of family is strong and loyal, and they live by carefully defined rules and rituals.

There seem to be specific territories that are sacred, and their social behaviors are based on a hierarchical structure. There is an alpha male and an alpha female that head the pack, though wolf packs aren't entirely autocratic—or democratic either. There are times when both occur, and it's this flexibility that adds to the success of the wolf government. Wolf teaches a balance between authority and democracy, and that freedom requires discipline. Wolf teaches both a strong sense of family within the pack and a strong individualistic urge.

The alpha male and female often mate for life, and when they breed, all members of the pack show much affection and care to the playful pups. Wolves are extremely tolerant, and if the parents aren't able to care for the pups, another member will adopt them. Some wolves will sometimes serve as babysitters. Adult wolves are amiable and friendly toward their pups, and Wolf medicine teaches respect and honor for family and children.

Wolves seem to love to howl, and do so for many reasons: to contact other pack members out of range of visual sighting, to announce their presence and boundaries of their territory, and for sheer joy. Baying at the moon may be an indication of Wolf's desire to connect us with new ideas that are just below the surface of consciousness. Wolf medicine empowers us to teach others what we have learned.

Wolves have stamina and strength that enables them to travel far, for extended periods of time. And wolves usually consume all that they capture, demonstrating the need to use all that is available. They teach us not to waste and remind us to keep our spirits alive.

Wolves are not only strong but very intelligent: they can outsmart hunters, even to the point of urinating on traps to show their distain. Wolf intelligence is also reflected in how wolves hunt—in relays, chasing the herd for long distances, during which they assess the weakest or eldest animals. There's nothing random about their selection. But when wolves hunt they will appear playful, lulling the herd into a false sense of security, as wolves assess which animals to take down. Thus, wolves have fun and take pleasure in all activities, exhibiting a spirit of joy even in work.

Wolves don't fight unnecessarily, and go out of their way to avoid trouble or danger. Some people believe that wolves use ravens as spotters, alerting them to danger or food sources. Ravens often follow wolves, then fly ahead, land in a tree, wait for the wolves to pass, and then fly on again. Wolf teaches us to know who we are and to develop strength, confidence, and surety so that we don't have to prove ourselves to others.

Wolves have keen senses, their sense of smell one hundred times greater than humans'. This sense endows them with great powers of discrimination, often associated with spiritual idealism in metaphysical circles. Wolves are said to ally with the moon, since the cones and rods in their eyes are adapted to see keenly in the dark. The wolf also has excellent hearing sensitivity, and Wolf teaches us to listen to our inner thoughts and words, helping us to be intuitive. Wolf teaches us discrimination and ingenuity.

For the Native Americans of Nootka Sound, the Wolf clan is one of the primary clans. The ceremony of initiation consists of a symbolic death (hunt) of the new initiate, who is reborn with the spirit of Wolf. The Niska people of British Columbia marked the initiate into the Wolf clan with symbolic death and resurrection.

The Shoshone believe that Wolf helped in creation and guards the path walked by the dead. Wolf awakens and washes the human soul in the river, thereby making it sacred, and then the newly cleansed spirit gains entry into the promised land. Thus, Wolf is associated with creation, death, the afterlife, resurrection, and rebirth—that is, transformation.

The wolf has a capacity for making quick and firm emotional attachments. Wolf helps us learn to trust our own insights and to secure our attachments accordingly. Wolf can help us hear the inner promptings and guards us from inappropriate actions. Wolf teaches us that it's time to breathe new life into our life rituals and to find a new path, take a new journey, and to take control of our life. We are the governor of our life and we create and direct it. If we do it with balance, harmony, and discipline, we will know the true spirit of freedom. But freedom doesn't come when we are slaves to our own erratic impulses and hastily conceived ideas.

In the Great Star Nation, Wolf is represented by the Dog Star, Sirius, which legend tells us is the original home of our teachers in ancient times. Wolf as teacher was so integral an idea to the Native American that in sign language used across the Plains—the Mississippi Valley and into the Rockies—the hand position for medicine (power) was nearly identical to that of the wolf.

Of all power animals, Wolf holds the role as teacher. Wolf teaches trust of self and a sense of identity, wisdom, and solidarity. Wolf also models courage and endurance and the warrior's skill to thrive. Wolf also teaches the power of discernment, to ferret out the truth in order to better define relationships and boundaries, while encouraging a sense of kinship and community. Wolf teaches us to learn our place in the social hierarchy. The pack works for the benefit of all, but in hunting, rest, and play, there is individuality.

Wolf has an innate ability for knowing when to retreat and when to attack, thereby anticipating right action, and its medicine imparts strength of character and integrity and bespeaks honoring lifetime commitments.

The attributes of Wolf include cunning, escaping hunger, ability to pass by dangers invisibly, outwitting those who wish to harm, and fighting only when necessary. Sometimes an astral Wolf will lead us to a spiritual teacher. Wisdom, hunting and seeking, intuition, listening, and protectiveness are all Wolf lessons. And Wolf can help us learn healthy love, forgiveness, intimacy, trust, community, selflessness, and generosity.

Since humans continue to expand their territory, wolves must move to wilder, less inhabited places, thus becoming a pathfinder. And as a pathfinder, Wolf is the forerunner of new ideas, returning to the clan to teach. Thus, we can call upon Wolf to guide us in our individual quests and to return to the clan to teach and share medicine. As pathfinder and protector, Wolf leads us, guides us, and gives us a sense of direction.

Raven. Though not identified as a Spirit Keeper of one of the Four Directions, Raven's ability to "partner up" with the wolf mimics the raven's role as a "familiar" for shamans and medicine people throughout the ages.

Legend has it that sometime in the past, Raven built its nest in the dimly lit loft of humanity's subconscious, and there it perches. Seeing its black silhouette in the sky, many of us recognize the shadow side of creation—flying out from time to time reminding us of what we have forgotten and what we still need to learn.

Raven is associated with magic, but can be associated with evil if sorcerers and black magicians misuse magic. Partly because of Raven's association with the Great Mystery, where all things are one and all things exist *in potentia*, Raven is equated with prescience, precognition, and prophecy.

Raven is the mark of the shaman, and its appearance signals a time for exploring and enhancing our power, helping us see deeply into the nature of reality and permitting us to move between the realms and pierce illusion. We can call upon Raven to give us courage to enter the darkness to seek the wisdom of the primal unconscious.

Raven grants us an understanding of the occult, of magic, and of exploring new and different aspects of our consciousness, which is the heart of magic—including healing magic.

Ravens are intelligent, adaptable, ingenious, and mischievous, and extremely noisy when disturbed. The Raven is an ambivalent bird connected with prophecy and wisdom. Zoroaster called it a "pure bird," and in Mithraism, the first grade of initiation was called the Raven. Raven is the guardian of ceremonial magic and *in absentia* healing.

Among some tribes, Raven plays the role of the Coyote: the trickster. Raven is intuitive and clever. Raven may trick us into getting out of our rut, to get us moving when we are being stubborn, resistant, or afraid of change. Raven is not only a trickster, but also a transformer: bending reality, working magic, and traveling astrally.

In ancient times, magic wasn't thought to be supernatural or paranormal, but rather it was the capacity to bring creative thought into physical reality. Raven may help us find inventive, creative, new solutions to old problems.

Raven magic helps us experience a change in consciousness, which may involve walking inside the Great Mystery on another path at the edge of time. Black can mean the seeking of answers, the void, or the road of the spiritual or nonphysical. Raven is the magic of darkness and changeability of form and shape that brings an awakening in the process.

When we are under the influence of Raven, we shouldn't try to "figure it out," but rather touch the power of the unknown at work; then something special might happen. The deeper mystery is how we will respond to the sparkling synchronicity of the alchemical moment.

Some tribes speak of the raven as the wisest of all the birds, and the first one to know all about the land. Raven is a spokesperson for the Great Spirit.

Cougar. Cougars are identified as the Spirit Keepers of the West in some traditions. The cougar is the second largest cat in the western hemisphere and one of the strongest and fastest—able to spring twenty to forty feet in one leap. Like other felines, the cougar has come to connote power, the feminine, and the intuitive. And the strength exhibited by the female in defense of her young demonstrates protectiveness and assertiveness. Cougar females are good mothers and fiercely protective of their young. But helping to care for the cubs may make a cougar powerful, but vulnerable.

Cougars can take down animals larger than themselves, including bears and wolves. And, interestingly, the female is the better hunter. But the giant feline never wastes anything and only kills to survive. The female cougar is the hunter who graces her table in a style akin to mother energy.

Cougar climbs higher than any other member of the cat family. Cougars are very much at home on the earth—grounded. For the Native American, Cougar represents leadership, physical grace, and strength. The Algonquian and Ojibwa know Cougar as a form of "underground panther" associated with the underworld. To the Cherokee, Cougar, along with the owl, is sacred because of its power to see in the dark.

Cougar exhibits intuitive ability, sensitive hearing, and night vision, and some say its medicine includes clairaudience or clairvoyance, which can be involved in seeking something hidden. Cougar also demonstrates patience and silence.

By observing the graceful pounce of the cougar, we can learn how to balance power, intention, physical strength, and grace. In human terms, Cougar balances mind, body, and spirit. And Cougar teaches us to look before we leap, but to take the opportunity and leap—to go for it if opportunity presents itself.

Cougar also teaches us the strength and self-confidence to stand up for ourselves and be assertive. When we begin to come into our power or begin to acknowledge that we have it, there may be people who discourage us—out of fear, envy, or competitiveness. Cougar helps us make the difficult choice when we know it's time to leap.

Cougar teaches us to stand on our convictions and lead ourselves where our heart takes us. Others may or may not choose to follow. Cougar medicine may ask us to review the purpose behind our personal beliefs. Cougar teaches us responsibility: the ability-to-respond to any situation.

The deer is the cougar's favorite prey, so anyone with Cougar medicine should study the deer in order to learn to balance power with gentleness. There are times to be assertive and times to be gentle; but there is strength in gentleness. The self-assured need not yell and bully in order to get someone's attention. Stubbornness, temper tantrums, and yelling are substitutes for strength and often occur if we feel out of control. Assertiveness may reflect a quiet strength and firmness.

Cougar's natural attributes are stealth, hunting and seeking, freedom, using power in leadership, balancing power, intention, and self-confidence. Cougar represents stealth, strength, and grace, with the attributes of assertiveness, maternal energy, and power. Cougar teaches about honing skills and learning a balance between power and intuition, physical strength and grace.

The Powers of the Four Cardinal Directions

The Powers of the Four Cardinal Directions are responsible for teaching Mother Earth's children about the spirit, meaning, and significance of each direction, the times, the seasons, the aspect of humans that each represents. The lessons are those of power in all its forms, and of the spiritual realms. And an element, stone, plant, color, time of day, month, moon, season, and a stage in our lives represent each Cardinal Direction.[21]

After offering the first pinch of tobacco to Father Sky and Mother Earth and the Spirit Keepers of the Four Directions, the pipe carrier reaches for a second pinch of tobacco. The second pinch is offered to Father Sky and Mother Earth. But having already called in and offered the Spirit Keepers the first pinch, with the second pinch the pipe carrier begins to call in other aspects of life on earth and the cosmos (always in multiples of four)—for example, the animal kingdom, plant kingdom, mineral kingdom, and sea kingdom. Starting in the East, each direction represents myriad features and characteristics to choose from.

East

The Powers of the Cardinal Direction of the East are associated with air, the mineral catlinite or pipestone, and the plant tobacco. Smoking tobacco can bring clarity, draw in energies, absorb negativity, and transform negative into positive energies.

The color of this direction is red, the color of dawn, and the color of the red race. The time of day is morning, the season is spring, and the stage of a person's life is childhood. The powers of the East are new beginnings, new growth for all of Mother Earth's children, freshness, newness, creativity. It is the time of bursting through, of the light that comes after the darkness, of the rightness we see after we have come out of the old. It is a time of rebirth, of all things possible, of innocence and of awakening. It brings the eternal promise of dawn and of spring, and knows that each moment can be a new beginning. Its gift is spontaneity, playfulness, wonder, inquisitiveness, and truth saying. It brings the abilities to explore, to feel high energy, or to be full of curiosity, to question everything, to see further and more clearly, to fly high, and to see things from a broader perspective.

In constructing the Medicine Wheel, one places the first stone in the center of the circle: the Creator stone. Then, in the Four Cardinal Directions, four stones representing the Spirit Keepers are placed in the East, South, West, and North.

Next, twelve more stones are added to the four—making sixteen stones—creating the outer circle. Twelve represents the twelve months of the year and the twelve moons. Completing the Medicine Wheel are twelve more stones, not including the Creator stone—made of up of three stones each radiating out from the Creator stones to the stones from each of the directions—connecting the Creator with the Spirit Keepers. These are four *Spirit Paths* where energy radiates in and out from the Creator stone—an ongoing, dynamic exchange and movement of energy. (See Figure 2.3.)

The three stones between the Eagle and the Creator are the *Spirit Path* representing *Clarity, Wisdom* and *Illumination.* The East is represented by the element of air and represents our mental aspect, and as pipe carriers offer a pinch of tobacco to the East, they pray for these three aspects of healing:

Clarity. On the mental level, Clarity allows us to see the truth, let go of lies, and use our own minds to discriminate and communicate clearly. Emotionally, Clarity helps us be more spontaneous, direct,

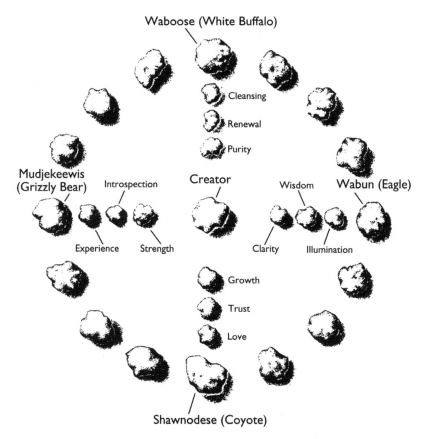

Figure 2.3. Medicine Wheel: Three stones on each path
radiate out from the Creator stone to a Power Animal.

smooth-flowing with unblocked energy. On the physical level, Clarity
helps us simplify our way of dealing with the world and live in a less
complicated manner. Spiritually, Clarity helps us become a more efficient
receiver and transmitter of universal energy.

Wisdom. On the mental level, this involves bringing the light of discernment into our minds in order to see deeper and higher. On the emotional
level it involves allowing ourselves to feel "lighter," to enjoy levity and
humor in our lives and to let the light of Spirit penetrate our hearts. On

the physical level, it involves feeling the light in our lives, feeling tingly and warm in all our relations. On the spiritual level, it involves letting the light of truth to illuminate our souls.

Illumination. On the mental level, Illumination helps us not only to grasp truth but to experience ourselves as truth. On the emotional level, Illumination helps us feel our truth in our own being, to live more authentically, and to work toward the experience of unconditional love. On the physical level, Illumination helps with the ability to let the sacred energy of the Creator flow freely and vitally through our bodies, helping us see the truth and light in our lives. On the spiritual level, Illumination helps us live the truth we have gained and it brings us to a divine understanding of life, to deeply know our connection with the universe, and to develop the capacity to radiate to others those truths we have learned.

South

The Powers of the South represent water, the mineral serpentine, and the plant sage. Burning sage is used to "smudge" the pipe and everything that touches it. Sage is to help drive out negative energies and to transform any energies that aren't working for the higher good of the person.

The color for the South is yellow, the color of one of the root races. It represents the midday sun and the stages of adolescence and young adulthood. The South brings the time of rapid growth, a time when every being has to reach out for fulfillment so quickly the youngster doesn't have time to question the path laid down by the Creator. This is the place where young people seek their visions and ask the Creator to point them in the direction they should go. Though they may plunge forth too rapidly sometimes, it is from the South that they receive the gifts of energy, adaptability, maturing, and playfulness.

This is a place to see the possible, to be open, outward, energetic, and changing. It is the place of the heart, of the emotions, a place to learn the power of love, sexuality, and openheartedness, but also discrimination.

The *Spirit Path* of the South represents our emotional aspect. As pipe carriers offer a pinch of tobacco to the South, they pray for *Growth*, *Trust*, and *Love* (which includes *Innocence*).

Growth. On the mental level, Growth is operating when we want to expand our knowledge and broaden and deepen ourselves. On the emotional level, it involves enriching our emotions, stretching, extending our boundaries, and expanding ourselves wider than before. On the physical level, Growth means change, development, unfolding, flowering, maturing, opening ourselves to more knowledge of the physical universe. Spiritually, Growth represents the harvest, evolution, and development of our spirit, becoming ready to take responsibility for our own life experiences.

Trust. On the mental level, Trust involves letting go of suspiciousness, wariness, and guardedness, and strengthening our belief in something or someone. It involves being mentally receptive rather than fearful and narrow-minded. On the emotional level, Trust involves increasing our capacity to receive and give love and to express ourselves more fully. On the physical level, Trust involves confidence in ourselves, accepting things, and being willing to surrender to life and sometimes to friends. Sexually, Trust involves opening up and becoming receptive, letting go. Spiritually, Trust involves living in such a way that we believe that the Creator loves and cares for us and isn't interested in punishing us; letting go and letting the Creator help us, trusting that the Universe is benign and loving and that the forces at work in the Universe are positive.

Love (including Innocence). On the mental level, Love involves finding out about healing emotional problems, learning how to communicate better, how to accept, and how to support ourselves and others. It involves learning about and practicing self-care and scheduling time for ourselves, learning more about honesty, honor, cherishing, and understanding. And returning to Innocence, we can go back to the "beginner's mind," to allow ourselves to be more childlike and experience wonder. Emotionally, we can learn about devotion, tenderness, compassion, and delight. And Innocence involves becoming more childlike in our authenticity, being direct and nonmanipulative. On the physical level, we can learn about pleasure, sexual energy, affection, touching, eating, smelling, tasting, looking with delight and pleasure, and feeling comfortable with sexuality, sensuality, and sensuousness.

Innocence, a human characteristic that supports love, helps us delight in the mundane, smell and appreciate the earth, feel awed by a sunset or cloud formation, to be playful, and to enjoy our bodies and how they move and work. On the spiritual level, Innocence helps us maintain a childlike trust in the Creator and the Universe and all the powers that are operating in it. It involves letting go and being receptive to synchronicities in life. And through love, we can understand the true meaning of devotion, transcendence, unconditional love, and acceptance. And we can learn about selflessness, service, and having the commitment and devotion to serve all our relations.

West

The Powers of the West are represented by the element of fire; the mineral is soapstone, and the plant cedar. Cedar is a strong plant, one that houses, nurtures, guards, and protects many of Mother Earth's children. Both the boughs and inner bark of the cedar are used ceremonially, and it is a cleansing and purifying plant and a strong healing agent. Native Americans use cedar bark for parts of houses, canoes, implements, clothing, and ceremonial items.

Its color is black, representing the black race, and the time of day twilight and the onset of night; the season is autumn, and the time of one's life is adulthood and maturity. It is during the time when all of Earth's children prepare to give their harvest back to the Earth Mother.

It's during this time that the seeds from the plants fall back into the earth in preparation for the seasons that will come. It's a time when people follow their vision, a time of experience, maturity, and expertise when people have found their abilities, skills, and knowledge and are ready to share them.

The *Spirit Path* of the West involves one's physical self, and when pipe carriers offer a pinch of tobacco to the West, they pray about *Experience*, *Introspection*, and *Strength*.

Experience. On the mental level, Experience involves learning through trial and error and remembering what we have learned and the mental habits that guide our learning. Emotionally, Experience brings us more stability, confidence, and involvement in our lives and our relationships. On the physical level, Experience means concrete skills, body memory, and learning something by putting our hands on it. Spiritually, we learn to be selective—if we wish to internalize the lessons we have been taught and are gaining through spiritual maturity—and to focus the knowledge we are gaining through life.

Introspection. Mentally, Introspection helps us reflect, contemplate, synthesize, and take stock of ourselves, think before we speak, and let our communication be guided by wisdom. Emotionally, we learn through Introspection what our true feelings and patterns are and how to integrate our emotions. On the physical level, we learn to retreat into solitude and quiet to learn from turning inward. On the spiritual level, Introspection helps us evaluate our spiritual ideas and experiences and become aware of the cycles of life and, in the stillness, get direct experience of the Creator and direct communication with the sacred energy within us and around us. We can find the truth of the Universe inside ourselves.

Strength. Mentally, Strength helps us have the courage of our conviction if we wish for more security or to become more focused, determined, and decisive. Emotionally, Strength involves becoming more centered, more self-aware, more balanced, and more courageous. On the physical level, Strength involves steadfastness, endurance, stamina, a steady flow of energy, and inner power. Spiritually, Strength helps us gain conviction when we explore various spiritual disciplines, and learn our true connection with Creator.

North

The Cardinal Direction of the North is represented by the element earth. Its mineral is alabaster, and its plant sweetgrass. Sweetgrass, known as "the hair of the Mother," attracts and draws in positive energies. It calls in and invites the good spirits to a ceremony. Like the buffalo who gives of itself, all of the sweetgrass except the roots is used in ceremony. The roots are left deep within the earth so that they can soak up the deepest earth energy and prepare themselves, at some point later, to give away their most special of gifts to all of their relations.

The color for this direction is white, representing the white race, the White Buffalo, the full moon reflected on the snows of the north, and the white hairs on an elder's head. The time of day is midnight, the season is winter, and the stage in a person's life is old age. It is a time when things seem to be sleeping, yet within the apparent dormancy, some of the deepest growth is occurring. Seeds lie frozen within the earth but take into themselves all of earth's energy that allows them to grow in the season that follows. It is a time for slowing down, a time of apparent restriction, when outward activity diminishes.

It's a time of darkness, quiet, and dreams, of human physical fragility, when skin wrinkles and resembles the soil and the face of the Earth Mother, a time when people tend to reminisce and share wisdom, a time of assessing accomplishments and aims, and of preparing for death and rebirth. It's a time of peace, power, forgiveness, and compassion, a time to give up old patterns and to surrender to the small changes of body and mind in preparation for the major changes to come.

The *Spiritual Path* of the North represents our spiritual aspect, and as pipe carriers offer a pinch of tobacco to the North, they offer it for *Cleansing, Renewal,* and *Purity.*

Cleansing. On the mental level, Cleansing involves clearing out old ideas and negative or self-defeating thinking patterns, or ideas or patterns that no longer fit or work in our lives. Emotionally, Cleansing involves discharging blocked emotions, ridding ourselves of emotional misconceptions, and opening ourselves to a wider vista of feelings. On the physical level, Cleansing involves detoxifying our body to get rid of impurities that interfere with our health. Spiritually, Cleansing may aid us in knowing what exactly is sacred to us and to surrender old spiritual ideas.

Renewal. On the mental level, Renewal helps us develop a healthy attitude about the way we view the world around us and our place in it, and to open up to new ideas or restructure our thinking and gain new perspective. On the emotional level, Renewal involves learning how to be good to and take care of ourselves in terms of our feelings. Physically, Renewal is what happens when we dedicate ourselves to becoming healthy and more fit, when we nourish ourselves and rebuild, revitalize, and replenish our bodies. On the spiritual level, Renewal is a result of getting in touch with the true foundation of our beliefs and formulating ceremonies to bring our spirituality into focus and renewing our belief in the Creator and in the goodness of all of life.

Purity. Mentally, Purity involves getting rid of preconceptions, misconceptions, and cynicism to see things in a non-jaded way—fresh, pristine—with the capacity to look at the world with the eyes of a child. Emotionally, Purity involves renewing our sense of integrity, being honest, spontaneous, and receptive. Physically, Purity involves living a wholesome life, eating right, and not contaminating our body with toxins: bad food, nicotine, and chemicals. And it involves returning to the innocence and enthusiasm of a child, giving up lying or manipulating, and becoming playful in our relationships. Spiritually, Purity involves coming into integrity with our beliefs and visions, and being clear and authentic in our spiritual practices.

* * *

By smoking the Sacred Pipe at the Medicine Wheel, we share breath with all of the four major powers of the universe and enter into communion with each spirit guide by sharing spirit (breath) through the pipe. We offer breath (life) in ceremonious acknowledgements to celebrate and to connect with the wisdom and power of each position on the Medicine Wheel.[22]

3

Ceremonies with the Sacred Pipe

Black Elk once said, "The power of a ceremony is the understanding of it." And the more we understand the pipe ceremony—or any ceremony—the clearer can be our intent, the more focused our participation, and the more profound our experience of the ceremony.

Any ceremony is a way for humans to give back to creation some of the energy they are always receiving. The Earth Mother constantly gives us two-leggeds a surface on which to place our feet. Father Sun warms and Grandmother Moon brings dreams. The element of earth gives us a place to grow food and the ability to make homes and tools. The water keeps us alive and fire warms our homes and cooks our food. Air gives us the sacred breath of life. So each part of the Medicine Wheel, each part of life, is constantly giving gifts to humans.[1]

A ceremony is a gateway into both spiritual freedom and spiritual maturity—an individual journey linked with awareness of the larger community. Through ceremony we learn to give back to Earth and to the Creator. We give energy with our voice; drumming mimics the heartbeat of the Earth; dancing brings the energy of Earth and Sky together in our bodies and gives it out. There is an old Native American saying: "We do not believe our religion, we dance it!" When we chant, we take Earth energy in through our bodies, magnify it, and send it out to all our relations on the planet. When we pray, we give energy through our hearts; and when we look upon our relations, we give blessings through our eyes. When we put all our activities together, we have a ceremony—one of our most positive forms of gift-giving.[2]

Native spirituality is mystical and mythic. But mystical experiences are first prepared for and conditioned by lifelong participation in a particular spoken language that hears sacred power through its vocabulary, structure, and categories of thought. Language serves as a vehicle for a large body of orally transmitted traditions—all the themes of which also express elements of the sacred. Such mystic experiences become more available to those who have participated with intensity and sincerity in a large number of exacting rites and ceremonies that have been revealed through time and derive from a transcendent source.[3]

Native tradition provides the means, essentially through sacred rites, for contact with and ultimately a return to the transcendent Principle— Origin, Source. Progress on such an inner journey demands the means for accomplishing the progression and integration of certain spiritual dimensions:

1. *purification* of body, soul, and spirit (sweat lodge);
2. *spiritual expansion*, by which individuals realize their totality and relationship to All That Is, and integration with, and realization of, all of reality and its virtues (vision quest, pipe, drumming, sun dance);
3. *identity*, or formal realization of *unity*: a state of oneness with the ultimate Principle of All That Is (all ceremonies).

Spiritual expansion is impossible without the prerequisite of purification, and ultimate identity is impossible outside the realm of virtue, wholeness, or spiritual expansion. These themes of *purification, expansion,* and *identity* are inherent in all the spiritual ways of the orthodox traditions of the world.[4]

The Sacred Pipe plays an important role in almost all Native American ceremonies, whether they are conducted alone or in community. Of particular interest here is the role the Pipe plays in the sweat lodge, the vision quest, and the sun dance.

SWEAT LODGE: RELEASE, CLEANSING, REBIRTH

Though the Sacred Pipe can be smoked alone, the sweat lodge usually involves a community of people. And it is a purification ceremony that is often undertaken in preparation for other rites and practices—such as the vision quest and sun dance.

Research suggests that the sweat lodge dates back to the ice age among Native peoples.[5] The lodge is shaped like the turtle, representing "Turtle Island" (North America). In the construction of a lodge, a hole is dug where heated rocks will be placed. This pit in the center of the lodge is the "heart of the turtle." A path of dirt (the "path of life" and "neck of the turtle") leads outside the lodge to a mound of dirt taken from the hole, which becomes the "head of the turtle," serving as an altar. A branch is often placed upright in the middle of the altar (the "Tree of Life") and the Sacred Pipe leans against it. Through the Tree of Life, the realm of the spirit and the everyday realm of the world are brought together. Beyond the altar, a large fire pit is dug to ceremonially heat the Stone People (the rocks) for the sweat lodge. Within the large fire pit will be the "eternal fire" or "fire of no end."

After tobacco is offered to each live willow (or ash, in some cases) the saplings are cut and stripped, to be used for the frame of the lodge. The willows that grow near water and bring the spirit of water to the lodge are a medicine tree. Medicine (such as modern-day aspirin) can be obtained from their bark. Willows die (lose their leaves) in winter and resurrect in spring, just as lodge participants symbolically die and are reborn in the sweat lodge.

Black Elk[6] says that the lodge represents the Great Spirit and the central pit is His navel. He points out that the willows that make up the lodge's frame mark the four quarters of the universe. And, thus, the whole

71

lodge is the universe in an image, and the two-leggeds, four-leggeds, and winged peoples and all things of the world are contained within it.

When the cut willows are stripped, planted in the ground, and lashed together with their own skin (bark) to create a dome-shaped frame for the lodge, they resemble a rib cage, the rib cage of the Mother. When covered with canvas and blankets (buffalo, bear, elk, or other animal pelts in earlier times), the covering becomes the skin of our Mother. The lodge itself becomes a living being, the Great Spirit, and the womb of our Mother.

The fact that the lodge becomes its own vortex of energy was driven home to me in the 1990s when a group of people helped me build a sweat lodge where I would conduct the ceremony at the Mother Earth Festival outside Madison, Wisconsin. While others stripped the saplings, I pounded stakes into the ground for the holes to put in the trees. Then I inserted the trees as the others curved them around to make the outer structure of the lodge. I had them lash the saplings together with the long strips of bark while I ceremonially laid the stones on the central fire. When the lodge was almost completely lashed together, someone suggested that I get my hand in and lash the last few joints. When I stepped into the lodge, I felt it as a powerful dome of energy even though it hadn't even been covered yet.

In a sweat lodge ceremony, heated stones from the fire outside the lodge are brought to the lodge door by the fire tender and then placed in the pit within the lodge. The stones represent steadfastness, immovability—everlasting, indestructible, enduring, ancient Stone People, who existed long before plant and animal life, are alive and have much to teach us about patience and wisdom. The fire has universal significance, representing the Sun, the molten core of Earth, and all the fires that have kept humans warm and cooked their food throughout the ages.

In the sweat lodge ceremony, we enter in ignorance into the dark, damp womb of the Mother and are smudged with cedar or sage. Cedar and sage, to remove negative energies, and sweetgrass to bring in positive energies, are also placed on the hot stones as they enter the pit within the lodge. The stones have specific placements within the pit and represent Mother Earth, Father Sky, Grandmother Moon, Grandfather Sun, the Star Nations, the Stone People, and other aspects of our universe.

At the beginning of each of the four rounds of the sweat lodge ceremony, the sweat lodge leader calls in each of the Four Directions, beginning with the Spirit Keepers and what they represent. Songs are sung and prayers are made for ourselves, others, our leaders, all our relations, and Mother Earth—for help, health, and healing. Depending on the tradition of the sweat leader, the Sacred Pipe may be smoked during each round, in just one of the rounds, in a fifth round with the door open, or after participants leave the lodge.

Fire (the sun) heats the stones, and water, the life-giving rain, is poured onto the heated stones. The sun's heat is in the glowing stones and brings forth our lifeblood—our water (sweat)—to mix with the lifeblood of the world, the ceremonial water that is poured on the stones from the leader's bucket. Water, the blood of the Mother, sings when it is poured onto the hot stones, becoming steam, the breath of the Mother, and mixes with our water—sweat and tears.[7]

The sweat lodge is both unique and archetypal. It is an ancient, almost universal, form of ceremonial purification, cleansing, and renewal. Its power moves through a primal, elemental process of transformation; the lodge is a timeless, sacred space where all worlds meet and all realms can be touched. The sweat lodge is a crucible where we learn to let go, a cauldron of rebirth, and the womb where we find new beginnings if we have the heart to release the past.[8]

Because the sweat lodge involves entering the womb and being reborn, it seems to be universally linked to stories and ideas of creation. When we are within the lodge, in the presence of the flowing lava stones, the steam rises as it must have risen from the molten surface of the earth when the first rain fell long, long ago.[9]

The water, as steam, carries the Thunder Beings that usually come in storms but also bring the rains that help things grow.[10] The misty, fire-heated steam covers us, bringing forth our own mist (sweat), and our universal lifeblood comes forth and intermingles with the misty waters of our brothers and sisters around us. We may see, within the heated stones, images that have waited since time immemorial. We are energized by Father Sky, energized by the fire, a gift from the trees that, in turn, gave of themselves—they whose life energy came from the Sun—a part of Father Sky.[11]

The sweat lodge is a cleansing and healing of mind, body, and spirit. The hot steam and change in temperature as the lodge door is opened and closed between rounds promote physical healing. The heat and darkness help break up old patterns of thinking and force us to turn inward, intensifying feelings and purging us of negative emotions. And the whole experience invites us to connect spiritually with others, the Earth, and ourselves.

When the sweat lodge ends and the door is opened for the last of the four rounds, as Black Elk puts it, "The light enters into the darkness, that we may see not only with our eyes, but with the one eye which is of the heart, and with which we see and know all that is true and good."

The light destroys darkness, just as wisdom drives away ignorance. Going forth into the light from the house of darkness, in which all impurities have been left behind, represents human liberation from ignorance, from the ego, and from the world. We are now a renewed being, entering symbolically into the world of light and wisdom.[12]

The sweat lodge tests our endurance and forces us to confront ourselves. As we crawl from the lodge, we realize we have undergone an ordeal of purification, cleansing, and renewal, and we return to the outside world as if reborn. The Sioux name for the sweat lodge is the *Inipi*, which means "to live again." We have experienced a symbolic death and rebirth, and now, hopefully, we can begin anew to live with renewed vitality and purpose.

VISION QUEST: AWARENESS, IDENTITY, DESTINY

Another Native ceremony that involves the Sacred Pipe is the vision quest. But far from being a goal achieved, the vision quest marks the beginning of the traditional Native American's lifelong search for knowledge and wisdom. Not a once-and-for-all phenomenon, the vision quest may be conducted whenever a Native seeks insight and wisdom or needs help with a particular problem.[13]

The vision quest is undertaken alone, usually after a sweat lodge, to seek a personal vision. The quester sits alone in the wilderness, without food and, among traditionalists, water also, for four days, with only a Sacred Pipe and a blanket, "crying for a vision." The seeker must enter the vision quest with a clear purpose and pure intent in order to insure a useful experience from the ordeal.

Most believe that quest intentions fall into two categories: prayer-questing, a time for addressing personal or larger concerns in an earnest and deeply engaged fashion; and alliance-questing, seeking powerful awareness of life's sacred web and the nourishing connections within it.[14]

The basic aim of the quester is to enter into the inner silence in order to embrace the outer silence. The purpose of the vision quest is to discover one's self—one's destiny, one's relation to the Earth, and one's medicine power—and to connect with the Creator.[15]

If a holy man or medicine man or woman is available, we may approach the leader with a filled Sacred Pipe and request that he or she be our guide. If the leader agrees, he or she will accept the pipe and smoke it. We may receive special instructions—for example, making tobacco ties or erecting colored flags for the Four Directions:[16] yellow for the East, red for South, black for West, white for North (in many traditions), blue for Father Sky, and green for Mother Earth.

To begin a vision quest, after a sweat lodge we go to the spot we have chosen for ourselves, and we may place sticks with colored flags, representing the colors of each of the Four Directions. We draw a circle on the earth around ourselves noting the Four Directions and center of the circle. The symbol of the Creator is the circle, and the movement of the Creator is in all directions. The directions vary and commemorate the seasons and the phases of sun and moon. But the center of the circle, the eye of the Creator, is motionless and unchanging.[17]

Then we make an offering to the Great Spirit with the Sacred Pipe. We offer a prayer, telling the "Great Silence" and its Four Powers who we are and what we seek, asking for their guidance and help. When not smoked, the Sacred Pipe may be held or placed in the center of the circle as an altar, where it is contemplated. For the four days, we contemplate each of the Four Directions while remaining in the circle. We may make tobacco ties and smoke the Sacred Pipe regularly.

Through the vision quest, we may achieve liberation from the concept of a legalistic God and open to a living relationship with an indwelling spirit—to a personal relationship with an omnipresent Creator. Alone for four days, we may contemplate our alienation, our separation, from ourselves, others, and the Source. We are "exposed" to the elements of nature and may have to deal with our fear and loneliness.

As soon as we complete the vision quest, it is valuable to have a guide to tell our vision to. Sharing an experience that is so immediate fixes it, not only in memory but in memory that has now begun to *shift* from what was actually felt and experienced.[18] We need to capture the true experience in all its immediacy.

Guides seldom interpret extensively after hearing an immediate experience. Much of what happens during a vision quest is meant to gradually unfold over time in the experiencer's understanding and relevancy. As questers, we may be left for some time with an intensity of focus that opens us to messages from Spirit (or that mirrors something from our own consciousness). There is great value in what happens in a state of heightened attention and receptivity, though we may not experience it at the time as a "vision."[19]

In one of the first vision quests I undertook, I was fortunate not to have high expectations. I sat and smoked my pipe, prayed, meditated, and did tobacco ties for three days, and "nothing" happened. That night I was a little anxious: would "anything" happen? Then I had a dream in which I helped an old woman and someone who seemed to be her daughter, who was carrying a baby. As they walked into their house, a limo pulled alongside me and the back window was lowered. Inside was an old man with light brown skin who looked like the old movie actor, Edward G. Robinson—long, wide mouth and lips. He commended me for helping the people, and the limo drove off.

Contemplating the dream the next day, I was looking at my "mesa," a circle of stones on a cloth I received from the Q'ero, medicine people who are the last of the Incas living in the high Andes mountains of Peru.[20] Similar to the American Indian Medicine Wheel, the mesa had an outer circle of twelve stones, four of which represented the Spirit Keepers of the Four Directions. As I stared at the stones, a tiny butterfly landed on the stone of the East and then flew off. A few minutes later, it flew back and landed on the South stone. After flying off and coming back a total of four times, the butterfly landed briefly on each of the Spirit Keeper stones in a sun-wise manner. Since the possibility of that happening by chance seemed about one in a billion, I felt blessed. It gave me the feeling that there was an underlying consciousness and order in the universe that even the tiniest butterfly participated in. When I later recounted the experience, my guide felt that the experience was sent to reinforce my faith in the process of life—that all of life participated in the same consciousness, the same Oneness.

I later met with a Peruvian shaman with whom I had been working for about six years, and I casually mentioned the man in the back seat of the limo in the dream. "Did he look like a frog—wide mouth pulled back, large lips?" "Yes. Why do you ask?" "That was one of my first spiritual teachers who is no longer on the earth plane," he explained. I had been visited by my teacher's teacher.

Through the vision quest we may discover our identity and destiny so that we can support the order of the universe in coexistence with creation. As John Redtail Freesoul puts it:

"The reward of the vision quest is the unending joy of deliverance and liberation from suffering through our communion of self with Source, the ultimate, unchanging Great Spirit. . . . As warriors, our vision and medicine power enable us to be strengthened by our adversaries, not intimidated by them."[21]

Through the vision quest, we may re-establish our sense of interconnectedness with all creation and reconnect with ourselves, our identity, and our destiny.

Sun Dance: Sacrifice, Renewal, and Freedom

Another ceremony that intimately involves the Sacred Pipe is the sun dance. But, whereas the vision quest is an individual activity, the sun dance is a tribal gathering: a beseechment, act of remorse, self-sacrifice, and thanksgiving. However, those who pledge to be sun dancers may do a vision quest in preparation for the sun dance. And they always undertake a sweat lodge ceremony before dancing.

Joseph Epes Brown states that the annual sun dance ceremonies of the Plains Indians give to these peoples—and to all peoples—a message through example, affirming the power of suffering in sacrifice, revealing in rich detail the mystery of the sacred in its operations, in all of life, and throughout all of creation. Where there is no longer affirmation or means for sacrifice—for making sacred—where the individual loses the sense of center, the very energy of the world will run out.[22]

The sun dance is an annual springtime world- and self-renewal ceremony that today is instrumental in preserving and revitalizing many traditional religious elements. The large, circular open-frame lodge is ritually constructed in imitation of the world's creation, with the sacred cottonwood tree at the center as the axis linking Sky and Earth. Some tribes, such as the Lakota, periodically move within the lodge in such a manner that the dancers are always gazing toward the sun—which is associated with the source of life.

The Sioux sun dance lasts four days. In earlier times, it was held after summer buffalo hunts, when the buffalo meat was cured and dried for winter provisions. It was a time of celebration and of plenty. Today the sun dance is more apt to be held in July or August.

To reconstruct from timbers the circular ceremonial lodge, the lodge of "new birth," "new life," and "thirst lodge," is to reenact the creation of world and cosmos. Horizontally, the lodge doorway situated in the east is the place whence flows life in light. At the center of the lodge, the sacred cottonwood tree, rooted in the womb of Mother Earth and stretching up out to the Heavens, represents the axis of the world and the male generative principle. Into and out of this central point and axis of the lodge flow the powers of the six directions. When men in ceremony are actually tied to this Tree of Center with the flesh of their bodies, or when women make offerings of pieces of flesh cut from their arms, sacrifice through suffering is accomplished so that the world and all beings may live, so that life may be renewed, so that human beings may realize their identity.[23]

At the sun dance, special persons are chosen for specific ritual functions. And they become what they personify: Earth Maker, Lodge Maker, and the venerable sacred woman of purity who is Earth herself in all her powers and with all her blessings. Without the presence of this most sacred woman, there can be no sun dance, for the duality of cosmic forces—the complementarity of male and female—are essential to the creative act and central to the realization of totality. To better translate cosmic realities and processes into immediate visible and effective experience, the bodies of participants are prayerfully painted with earth colors the forms of sun, moon, stars, hail, lightning, and various elements of nature.[24]

At certain times, special altars are constructed upon the earth; the means of construction is simple, but their importance is profound. A place on the earth is cleared and made sacred, directions of the world are delineated, always in reference to the center; humanity's relationship to the cosmos is established, its true "path of life" defined. Ceremonial Pipes, themselves portable altars, are ever present with these earth altars. There is an association between the straight pipe stem and the central sacred tree: both are axes, both trace the Way and express the male generative principle, and both speak of sacrifice.[25]

Dancers wear and use their whistles made of the wing bone of an eagle to which eagle plumes are attached. In re-creating the cry of the eagle in the powerful rhythm of song, dance, and drum, the eagle is present in voice and being. A human being's vital breath is united with the essence of the sun and life. Through such ritual use of sacred form, a human becomes an eagle, and the eagle with its plumes is the sun. At each morning's greeting of the new sun, dancers face the east holding their eagle plumes toward the sun's first ray, bathing the plumes in the new light of life, then placing the plumes in movements of purification of the head and of all parts of the upper body, while dancing to the rhythm of heroic song. Dignified movements of dance facing the sun of the sacred tree are sustained in the suffering of thirst, day and night, through the beat of the drum, the heart and life of the world, now one with humankind's own heart and life.[26]

I have summarized a description of the Sioux sun dance by Ed McGaa (Eagle Man), Oglala Sioux author of *Mother Earth Spirituality*:[27]

On the day before the first ceremony day, a felling party goes out and finds a cottonwood tree, and a woman representing White Buffalo Calf Maiden takes the first cut of the tree with an ax. The cottonwood tree is planted in the center of the arena. But before the tree is raised, a Sacred Pipe is placed in a hole dug for the tree trunk. In earlier times, buffalo tallow was also placed in the hole to acknowledge the rich provisions given by the buffalo to the people.

Cloth banners in the colors of the Four Directions are tied to the branches with green and blue banners for Mother Earth and Father Sky. Above the long bolts of cloth, a cutout of rawhide is made in the form of a buffalo and tied with a rawhide cutout of a human image. Twelve chokecherry branches are tied crosswise beneath these cutouts. The branches symbolize the twelve moons—the twelve months of the year. And the cutouts represent thankfulness. The tree is raised, and the camp area springs to life with new arrivals.

In the evening of the tree moving, a sweat lodge ceremony is held for the people who have pledged to be sun dancers. Pledges usually take their vows the preceding year and live their lives for that year in the best possible manner, avoiding disharmony and striving to conduct themselves in an appropriate manner. In the sweat lodge, pledges restate their vows.

The first day of the sun dance begins in the very early morning with two sweat lodge ceremonies, one for males who missed the night before and one for the females. Afterwards the sun dancers dress for the sun dance, and each carries an eagle bone or wooden whistle and a Sacred Pipe.

On the second day of the sun dance, the sun dancers present their Sacred Pipes to the man or woman who accepts them. If there are many dancers, they may be broken up into four groups, each facing one of the Four Cardinal Directions. Each dancer is then brought before the acceptor, a woman flanked by two holy men. As each Sacred Pipe is accepted, it is placed beyond the buffalo skull that is resting on the ground. The skull, with its curved horns, is placed in front of a pipe rack for the Sacred Pipes. Holy men address the crowd about the importance of the sun dance; and dancers gather around the pole contemplating knowledge, wisdom, peace, and harmony. They may ask that the ignorance, fear, and egocentricity that hold them back from enlightenment be removed. The third day is similar to the second.

On the final day, each sun dancer lies on the ground while a blade or sharp skewer is used to make two parallel cuts on the dancer's chest and an awl is thrust into the first cut and out the second. A peg, pointed on one end, is then placed through the incisions and the holy man wraps a leather thong around the projecting ends of the pegs and ties the thongs to the rope that is tied to the Tree. The dancer's ropes are the umbilical to the Mother Earth.

When the dance begins, the bone whistles screech and the drums pulse louder. Dancers dance inward to touch the Tree of Life, the great cottonwood. They lean against the trunk and then back away slowly, shuffling with the drumbeat to the end of their tethered connection. The tree is touched four times, and then they lean back against the ropes—free to seek their sun dance vision. And people in the crowd seek their own vision. Eventually, for each sun dancer, the peg tears through the skin, and the dancer is released.

Joseph Epes Brown explains:

> The sun dance is not a celebration by humans for humans; it is an honoring of all life and the source of all life, that life may continue, that the circle be a cycle, that all the world and humankind may continue on the path of the cycle of giving, receiving, bearing, being born in suffering, growing, becoming, returning to the earth that which has been given, and finally being born again. Only in sacrifice is sacredness accomplished; only in sacrifice is identity found. It is through suffering in sacrifice that freedom is finally known and laughter in joy returns to the world.[28]

4

Native American Spiritual Philosophy

Tom Brown, Jr., the world's foremost survivalist teacher and long-time apprentice to the Apache tracker and medicine man Stalking Wolf, eloquently expresses the need for the beginner's mind in approaching Native American spiritual philosophies:

> The spiritual world is a world to which the seeker comes slowly—first with the faith of a child, then with the patience and dedication of a sage. It requires one to let go of all beliefs, all prejudices, and all need for scientific methods of verification. One must abandon logical thinking and learn to deal in the abstract, learn to accept that each moment is an eternity, and that each entity becomes, at once, a physical and spiritual teacher.[1]

NATIVE AMERICAN COSMOLOGY

In order to understand Native American spirituality, it is necessary to know how Natives perceive and conceptualize the cosmos.

Consciousness and Our Cosmic Origins

The path of consciousness for humans is an unfolding of embodied spirit. If we think of consciousness as something we participate in rather than something we have, our whole perspective shifts; we see the spiritual nature of ourselves and everything in the cosmos. Consciousness expresses itself and is embodied in the web of life and the complexity of all of its manifestations. Each manifestation—stones, bears, birds, trees, humans—carries the light of its cosmic origin, the potential within the Mind of the Great Mystery. Awakening to Spirit's presence through our moment-to-moment opportunities for connection within the web gives impetus and direction to our homeward yearnings—as we follow our path toward self-knowing.[2]

According to some Native teachers, the individual soul is created as an extension of the Great Spirit and is a reflection of the Creator's consciousness. The soul is light, which evolves and matures into the likeness of the Creator.[3]

The ancient ritual of the Sacred Pipe requires a specific cosmological understanding—view of the cosmos—that continues into the present time. We can gain an understanding of the underlying cosmology of Native peoples by understanding the Medicine Wheel and analyzing the movements of the Sacred Pipe ritual.

Native Americans' Personal Experience of the Cosmos

Since it flows directly from personal experience, Native spirituality is open to continual revelation from Spirit. Hence, Native theology is flexible and able to respond rapidly to changing circumstances without altering its fundamental characteristics. Revelation takes place during a person's lucid dreams, visions, and prophetic experiences, through rituals like the Sacred Pipe, sweat lodge, vision quest, or sun dance. And since continuing revelation takes place within a mythic and ritual context, it maintains rather than disrupts spiritual continuity.[4]

The classical dwelling of Plains people is the portable, conical teepee, which expresses cosmological and metaphysical meanings. The teepee, sweat lodge, dream lodge, and sun dance circle are understood as the universe or, microcosmically, as a human being. The central fire of the teepee is the presence of the Great Mysterious, which is at the center of all existence; the smoke hole at its peak is the place and *path of liberation*.

At the sun dance, the large, circular open-frame lodge is ritually constructed in imitation of the world's creation, with the sacred cottonwood at the center as the axis linking Sky and Earth. Dancers move from the circumference to the tree at the center and back, always facing and concentrating upon the tree at the center. So the dancers are always gazing toward the sun, which is associated with the *source of life*.

The concept of the vertical axis explains the sacredness of the number seven, consistent with other world religions. In adding the vertical dimensions of Sky and Earth to the four horizontal ones of space, we have six dimensions, with the seventh as the point at the center where all the directions meet and where the person or people gather.

To realize this symbol in its fullness we must conceive of three horizontal circles inscribed with crosses, all three pierced by the vertical axis of humanity itself. The human being is the intermediary between Sky and Earth, linking the two, with feet on the ground and the head at the center of the firmament. The middle disk, like the vertical axis, represents humanity; for in joining Sky and Earth, it is neither pure spirit nor gross matter, but a synthesis of both. The Crow tribes often paint three rings around the cottonwood tree at the center of the sun dance lodge—the circles representing the three "worlds" they believe constitute human beings: body, soul, and spirit.

Cycling of Time

Historically, linear concepts of time are of relatively recent origin. They emerged with certain Judaic perspectives but didn't become pervasive in the Western world until the beginning of the European Renaissance. They then intensified with the rapidly changing ideologies of the Reformation. But when we are oriented toward both past and future, we are distracted from the human and spiritual possibilities inherent in the *fullness of our being in the now.* Living in the moment allows us to be in *immediate and continuing relationships* with the qualities and forces of our natural environment.

Implicit in the Western mind's notion of time is that "process" is now identified with "progress," moving onward and upward—mostly upward. But the process of change inherent in nature is cyclical and not linear. In the primordial tradition, people celebrate the grand mysteries of the cosmos through *seasonal,* thus *cyclical,* rites and ceremonies—supported by rich and varied forms of art, architecture, music, and drama.

Seeing life as a process opens it up to being *immediately observed* and *experienced* in all the forms, beings, forces, and changes of nature. At the center of all change, as at the center of all phenomena, is the indwelling Presence of ultimate Mystery. And at that center, we partake of and are surrounded by the Totality of All That Is.

All the forms and beings of nature are held as sacred and thus treated with respect. The Native Americans' reverence for nature and for life is central to their spirituality. The rhythm of the cycles of the cosmos, the sun, and the seasons repeats the cycle of human life as it moves from birth to death and to rebirth.

But change can have neither meaning nor purpose unless it is in relation to the *changeless,* which is at the center of every circle or cycle. The world of appearances has neither reality nor message for the realization of the fullness of our humanity unless it is understood in relation to the *Absolute.*

If animistic beliefs—consciousness and even sacredness in nonhumans—are understood as being ultimately attached to a universal Principle, then we realize that the mysteries of the *creative process* are witnessed through every form and force of nature and immediately experienced in the now.

Power of Place

Native American experiences of place are infused with mythic themes that express events of sacred time, which are as real now as at any other time. They are experienced through landmarks in each person's immediate natural environment. The events of animal beings, for example, which are communicated through oral traditions of myths and folklore, serve to grace, sanctify, explain, and interpret each detail of the land.

Native Americans experience every being of nature and particular form of the land as being infused with many different spirit beings—ancestors, guides, totem animals—whose individual and collective presence sanctify and give meaning to the land in all its details and contours. Sites, stones formations, buttes, and animal behavior in a particular area may be important and sacred. Thus, it also gives meaning to the lives of people who can't conceive of themselves apart from the land.

Such affirmation and experience of sacred time and sacred place free people from everyday appearances so they can be thrust into a deeper and more profound sense of the sacred dwelling beneath. The teepee or longhouse—like the temple or the cathedral of antiquity—determines the perimeters of space in such a way that a sacred place, or enclosure, is established. Space so defined serves as a model of the world, of the universe, or, microcosmically, of a human being.

The sacred cottonwood tree at the center of (and branching out above) the Plains sun dance lodge is its central axis. It symbolizes the *way of liberation* from the limits of the cosmos. Vertical ascent is impossible unless the starting point is the ritual center.

Relationships

Relationships between members of family, clan, or tribal groups are defined and intensified through relational or generational terms, rather than through personal names, which are considered to be sacred, and thus private, to the individual. This sense of relationship extends outward to include all beings of the specific environment, the elements, and the wind—whether these beings or powers are animate or inanimate.

Native American Theology

Native American traditions have been developing on this continent for 100,000 years or more. Actually, the universally held theory that people came across the Bering Strait about 12,000 years ago was seriously challenged by Drs. Jeffrey Goodman, William Irving, James Bischoff, and John Bryde, along with Louis Leakey who reported carbon-dated bones found in North America that were 150,000 and 200,000 years old.[5] The oldest "statue" in the world of the Earth Mother—made of clay and in a reclining position—may date back from 282,000 to 800,000 years.

The ancient primordial traditions served as a foundation for formal religions that were developed many thousands of years later. Even the ancient Egyptians and the rishis, the sages from the forests who began an oral tradition that wasn't written down by Hindus until about 1500 BC, came thousands of years after humans had developed a spiritual impulse and began developing their legends, stories, and myths.

Many and the One
Native American spiritual traditions represent a form of theism (belief in a god) wherein concepts of both monotheism (one) and polytheism (many) intermingle and fuse without being confused. Among the western Lakota and eastern Dakota of the Plains, for example, the term *Wakan Tanka*, the Great Mysterious, is an all-inclusive concept that refers both to a Supreme Being and to the *totality* of all spirits or powers of creation. Such conceptualizations embracing both *unity* and *diversity* are typical of the *multiple* and *unifying nature* of the languages of these Native peoples.

In *The Vision*, Tom Brown, Jr., quotes the Apache tracker and medicine man Stalking Wolf in his beautiful description of the Great Spirit as "the-Spirit-that-moves-in-all-things."[6]

Joseph Epes Brown, in *The Spiritual Legacy of the American Indian,* reminds us that although these natural forms—animals and other beings—may reflect aspects of the Great Spirit, they are nevertheless not identified with He "who is without Parts" and who in His transcendent unity is above all particular created forms.

Black Elk explains that all created beings are sacred and important, for everything has an influence through which we may gain a little more understanding if we are attentive. For Black Elk, all things are the works of the Great Mystery: He is within all things—the trees, the grasses, the rivers, the mountains—but He is also above all these things and people.

The contemporary Navajo artist Carl Gorman said that he heard some Navajo religion researchers say that Natives have no Supreme God, because He isn't named. But Gorman insists that this is not so. The Supreme Being is not named because He is not knowable, but is simply the Unknown Power. He says that Natives worship Him through His creation, that Natives feel too insignificant to approach directly in prayer that Great Power that is incomprehensible to humans.

Gorman goes on to very poetically explain that for Natives, "Nature feeds our soul's inspiration." He says that Natives approach God through that part of Him which is close to them and within the reach of human understanding—because this great unknown power is everywhere in His creation. The various forms of creation have some of this spirit within them, just as every form has some of the intelligent spirit of the Creator. So Natives cannot but reverence all parts of creation.[7]

Natives don't fragment experience into mutually exclusive dichotomies, but stress *interrelatedness* across categories of meaning, never losing sight of an ultimate whole. For them, even rocks have life and consciousness. This type of ultimate affirmation of a Supreme Being was held centuries before the coming of whites and missionaries to America.[8]

This mode of interrelatedness leads to the perception of an underlying unity among many different kinds of phenomena. For example, a unifying element among spiders, rocks, trees, wind, and breath—all seen as powerful and helpful, fully natural spiritual beings. Yet for many Natives, there is no absolute distinction between Creator and created. All beings are relations; hence, the spirits, including animals, plants, and minerals, are all addressed as "Grandfather" and "Father," "Grandmother" and "Mother," as expressed in the prayer: "All my relations."

Though the Native Americans may invite or invoke the Fathers and Grandfathers or the Mothers and Grandmothers, they are praying to one Creator under His/Her various aspects. Joseph Epes Brown points out that in the language of the Lakota, for example, the Great Spirit may be referred to as either Father (*Ate*) or Grandfather (*Tunkashila*). Ate refers to the Great Spirit in relation to His creation—as *manifest* Being. Whereas Tunkashila is the *unmanifest essence*—the Source, independent of the limitations of creation. And Lakota differentiate between Mother and Grandmother: Mother is the Earth, considered as producer of all growing forms, *in action*. Whereas Grandmother refers to the ground or substance of all growing things—*potentiality*.

Native Americans believe that humans were created last of all the creatures, but we are also the "axis," and thus in a sense the first. For if each animal reflects particular aspects of the Great Spirit, human beings may include within themselves all the aspects. A human being is a totality, bearing the universe within him- or herself and, through the intuitive mind, we have the potential capacity to live in continual awareness of this reality.

Native Americans believe that such knowledge cannot be realized unless there is perfect humility: unless human beings humble themselves before the entire creation, before the smallest ant—realizing their own nothingness. Only in being nothing may an individual human being become every thing and only then realize the essential kinship with all forms of life. A human's center, or life, is the same center or Life of All That Is. The ego serves as a barrier to oneness. When that barrier dissolves, consciousness is free to experience oneness with the Great Mystery.

Mystery of the Winds

There's a deep mystery in the wind, since it is intangible and visible only through its effects. The Four Directions are the "homes" of the Four Winds, representing an immaterial God whose substance is never visible. There is a qualitative and comprehensive science of the winds among Native peoples: the winds' ultimate unifying principle is that it moves or exerts power over nature, for example, leaves, branches, bushes, and yet itself is unseen.

The Great Spirit is *wakan* (sacred) and a mystery and, therefore, no human can comprehend Him. While He is one God, He is four individuals—the idea of the four coalesces into a single Wind principle: Wakan Tanka. All wakan beings coalesce, or rather fuse into the One, linking and integrating a multiplicity of forms within a unifying concept. And so it is with the Great Mysterious, whose unseen presence gives life and movement to All That Is.

Power of the Symbol

To the Plains Indian, the material form of the symbol is not thought of as *representing* something other than itself, some higher realm, but *is* that reality in an image. Meanings generally are *intuitively sensed* and not secondarily interpreted through analysis. There tends to be a unity between form and idea or context. Here the "symbol" is, in a sense, that to which it refers. The tree at the center of the sun dance lodge does not just represent the axis of the world, but *is* that axis and is the center of the world; the sun is not a symbol of the Creative Principle, but *is* that Principle as manifested in the sun. A power animal painted on a shield doesn't represent an animal but *is* really present there and radiates toward all participants at a ceremony.

Quasi-naturalistic representation may have been used for special circumstances, but abstract representation is more prevalent. For in just a single aspect of a depicted being—in the paw of a grizzly bear or a painted image of an elk track—the *full force of the entire being* is presented and experienced. An animal or a vision-being painted on a shield or the cover of a lodge is understood to be *really present* with the fullness of its particular spiritual powers, which may be transmitted to the observer.

Traditional art forms are not experienced as symbols of some other agreed-upon referent. A spiritual essence of power specific to the particular form is present in an *immediacy of experience.*

Basket makers gathering grass and weaving is a ritual reenactment of the total process of creation. The completed basket *is* the universe in an image; and in the basket-making process, the woman actually plays the part of the Creator. In weaving a blanket, a Navajo participates in an act that imitates the creation of the universe itself. The quill worker is aware of the identity between the porcupine and the sun, and that the sun is a manifestation of the Creative Principle. The quill worker, laying out the quills in a geometric patterns established by tradition, is really *creating* rays of the sun; she "traps" the sun—understood as a spiritual principle—upon a garment.

When a person smokes a Sacred Pipe, the flow of breath is drawn from the source of life in the central fire-containing bowl, and when the bowl is carved with an animal being facing the one who smokes, a circular relationship, by means of visual image and shared breath, is established.

And as is generally the case with peoples close to their primal sources, the total world of experience is seen as being *infused with the sacred.*

Power of Myth
Defining the concept of a myth, scholar Ananda Coomaraswamy says: "The Myth [is] the penultimate truth, of which all experience is the temporal reflection. The mythical narrative is of timeless and placeless validity, true nowhere and everywhere. . . . Myth embodies the nearest approach to absolute truth that can be stated in words." He adds, "Myth is to history as Universal is to particular."**9**

Creation occurs not just once, out of nothingness in linear time past, but is an event ever *occurring and recurring* in cyclical fashion. As with each form of creation, the mystery of this creative cycle of birth, life, death, and rebirth is *immediately and continually manifest*. The Native myth tells us that certain beings, already created, participate and cooperate with the Creator in the act of creation. For the Native American, creation is not understood as a single event of time—but as an *immediately experienced process* of creation *ever happening and observable* through all the multiple forms and forces of creation.

To construct the circular ceremonial lodge, the lodge of "new birth," "new life," the "thirst lodge," from timbers brought from the mountains is *reenacting the creation of world and cosmos*. Horizontally, the lodge doorway situated in the East is the place whence flows life in light; from the South comes growth in youth; from the West ripeness, full fruit, and middle age; and from the North completion and old age leading to death, which leads again to new life.

In the Native myth, the Creative Principle itself is not locked into some separate time-space orientation; creation is an *eternal, ongoing process of the here and now*, in which what is created continues to participate.

Since time and the rhythm of life are experienced as cyclical and circular, processes transmitted through oral traditions are seldom recounted in terms of time past or time future in the linear sense. Actually, Native American languages don't have past and future tenses; they reflect rather a *perennial reality of the now*. Therefore, the rich mythic accounts of creation, for example, don't tell of chronological time past, but of processes that are *eternally occurring*.

Power of Words

Native American languages are joined to other sacred languages of the world in the sense that words are not just symbols assigned arbitrarily to other units of meaning. Rather, words in themselves are experienced in an *immediate manner* as laden with power. Thus, to name a being or an element of creation is actually to make *manifest* the power or quality, soul or spirit of that which is being named.

Pronouncing the word or name mysteriously makes present the *essence or power* of what is named. This power is enhanced by understanding that speech is borne by the breath, and breath comes from the area of the heart, understood as the spiritual center of the living being. Author of Native American lore Dennis Tedlock poetically states that it is the breath, universally identified with the essence of life itself and proceeding from the center of a person's being nearest the heart, that bears and fashions the word.[10]

When Native Americans end a story, they bring the listeners from mythic time to the present by relating and integrating the one into the others with "so that's why," for example, "the beaver has a long tail" or "to this day the maiden continues to weep for her lover"—thus creating an *experiential immediacy*.

Native Perceptions of Reality
The Oglala and many other tribes have an ability to organize categories of power or phenomena into generalized sets, freeing them to perceive and experience the world with less rigid limits than the one experienced by the non-Native. There is a *fluidity* and *transparency* to their perceptions of the world that permit no absolute line to be drawn. For example, no clear line is drawn between the worlds of animals, men, or spirits. Outward forms are conceived to be *shifting*, and some may be receptive to humans.

Time itself takes on the nature of a nonfragmented continuum. But the Native's world is neither unstructured nor chaotic, for underlying the fluidity of appearances, there is the binding thread of the wakan concept. An ultimate coalescence of the multiple into the unifying principle of Wakan Tanka does not compromise an essential unity. The world of the Oglala, for example, is a *spiritualized world* in which phenomena are affirmed for what they are and never disconnected from underlying principles.

Arnold Toynbee, the great historian of Western civilization, in the last piece of writing before his death—in *The New Yorker* in 1973—said:

> For pre-monotheistic man, nature was not just a treasure trove of "natural resources." Nature was, for him, a goddess, "Mother Earth," and the vegetation that sprung up from the earth's surface, the animals that roamed, like man himself, over the earth's surface, and the minerals hiding in the earth's bowels all partook of nature's divinity. The whole of his environment was divine.[11]

The correspondences between levels of reality are as if one were the reflection of the other; they flow into each other in a manner that expresses a totally integrated environment. And everything has a spirit. Further, everything in this dimension has a counterpart in a different dimension—the one we call the realm of the spirit.[12]

"All my relations" is a saying that recognizes all creation and the Creator as one great family. It extends kinship to everything "that lives and moves and has its being." Nothing can happen to part of this creation that does not in some small way happen to the rest of creation and its Creator. Everything forms a great web of interdependence, giving daily, even second by second, what is needed to keep everything alive. The spider web can serve as a parable for our minds to dwell on—likening the web to the family. Everything is interwoven and interdependent. If one part is unraveling, then it begins to weaken the rest of the web. All creation is one, is harmonious and holy. Every part needs to be reverenced as holy and worthy of respect so that it can have the freedom to carry out its duties and functions.[13]

THEOLOGY OF THE PIPE CEREMONY:
EMBRACING THE COSMOS

"With the smoking of the first Sacred Pipe, the ancient Native American elders of this continent discovered in spiritual communion that to share breath is to share life." So says John Redtail Freesoul, pipe maker, teacher, and author of *Breath of the Invisible*. Freesoul views the Sacred Pipe as a ceremonial tool and a traveling altar. Leaning against a forked peg pressed and anchored in the earth, the Sacred Pipe becomes a center of focus and concentration—an altar.

Freesoul goes on to state: "[The Sacred Pipe] is the center of all we do; it is the 'axis mundi' which forms a bridge between Earth and Sky, the visible and the invisible, the physical and spiritual."[14]

The pipe ritual *centers* on the Sacred Pipe itself. As the pipe is passed around the *circle*, the center passes with it. The pipe is always at the center of the cosmos. The smoke is offered in all directions, radiating outward from the Sacred Pipe. The bowl of the Sacred Pipe is a sacrificial vessel that itself is a miniature cosmos. Tobacco is offered pinch by pinch to the sacred directions as well as to the elements, the plant and animal kingdom, the star kingdom, the human kingdom, the Earth and Sky—as part of our relations—bringing the entire cosmos into the bowl.[15]

The stem of the Sacred Pipe, sometimes decorated on older pipes with a striped design symbolic of the trachea, directs the offering toward Sky and Earth—to the Great Spirit and the Earth Mother. The cosmos surrounding the Sacred Pipe is spherical rather than circular or hemispheric. The offerings are directed toward the Four Cardinal Directions, the zenith, and the nadir.[16]

The stem can be made from several types of wood: almond, hazel, ash, cottonwood. Well-known anthropologist Vinson Brown says that the stem is often made of cottonwood "because it is a wood that echoes the voice of the waters which are always near where this tree grows and where the Voice of the Great Spirit is heard when the wind whispers and murmurs in its leaves." And the clear channel of the hole in the stem symbolizes the open hearts and minds we must have to let the Spirit truly reach us."[17]

Frequently attached to the Sacred Pipe—usually to the stem—are the skin or teeth or bone of an animal, especially the buffalo—the symbol of the gift of food from the Great Spirit. Sometimes attached to the Sacred Pipe are feathers of a bird, especially the eagle. As Vinson Brown puts it, ". . . in the feel of these feathers and the skin of the animal we draw strength and wisdom from other life than that of humankind; we find kinship with them and can use their powers if we are wise."[18]

The pipe bowl is Earth Mother, the stem Sky Father. The bowl is the Earth, while the stem is all that grows on the Earth. The bowl is each person's head; the stem is the spine.

Medicine Man Wallace Black Elk said:

> Our Chanunpa [Sacred Pipe] consists of a stone and a stem. That stone is the female, the woman. Her blood ran into the ground and formed that red stone. That stem is male. It is also the Tree of Life. When the two are connected it produces the generation of life.[19]

The pipe stone is red, a color of great significance down through the ages. It symbolizes the color of the earth, the color of blood—the blood that was shed at Pipestone, the blood of the buffalo, and all of the blood shed by humankind through the ages. And it is the color of the red-skinned peoples.

Long before the rise of Western civilization, when the white man was still a barbarian, the civilized people of Africa and Asia Minor, Egyptians and Aryans, considered themselves part of the red race and were proud to belong to it. Egyptians used henna to stain their bodies a deeper red and painted an exaggerated shade of red on human forms in all their pictures.[20] And it seems that red has symbolized the life force for over fifty thousand years, as evidenced by Neanderthal burials.[21]

The reddish-brown stone bowl can represent the red-brown skin of Mother Earth and the durability and lasting quality of rock.[22] Vinson Brown challenges: "Look at a large and hard rock and visualize the strength in it, the hardness of it, and its everlasting nature, for it has probably been much as it is now for millions of years." Compare the shortness of our lives to the beginning of creation. Yet as short-lived humans, we can partake of that age and durability if we make our hearts one with the universe and purge away all the petty desire and vices that limit our vision.[23]

Brown further suggests, "The circle of the bowl of the pipe becomes to the user the Circle of the Universe, the Circle of Earth and its Life, and the Circle of Mankind."[24]

For some, the flesh and blood is the bowl; the bones are the stem. The bowl may represent the earth and the mineral world; the burning herbs or tobacco (fire) and the stem may represent the plant world; the attached skins of the four-leggeds of the Earth and feathers of the wingeds of the air are from the animal world. The smudge bowl, usually a shell, represents the animals of the sea kingdom; our saliva, the element of water. The four colors, sometimes represented in or attached to the stem, represent the four races of the two-leggeds.

Evelyn Eaton, beloved medicine woman, says that whenever the pipe head is joined to the pipe stem for the purpose of sacred ceremony, all the elements are present: tobacco represents the vegetable world; and the ascending smoke (combining the elements of air and fire) and the pipe head (clay), combining earth and water, represent the relationship between Earth and Heaven, the path through fire to transmutation.[25]

Coming Together

We can see the pipe stem as Sky Father—that which is the absolute, unchanging, unmanifested invisible spirit. In the wheel of life and in the hub of motion, there is always stillness in the center. The center is a concentration of the power of all the directions. There is a time appropriate for each of us individually, and sometimes collectively, as families, clans, tribes, to withdraw from the wheel of motion in life and go to the center of the hub—to get centered and become focused.[26]

The manifested, ever-changing spirit becomes visible as nature in Mother Earth, represented by the bowl. The bowl aids in recalling to mind acceptance of change in nature: Although we are in a sea of constant flux and change, there is always warmth, order, and beauty in nature. When our lives are in harmony with other lives (our relatives), and if our will and behavior are in balance with the sustaining natural law (order) of the Creator, then we perceive and directly experience this warmth, order, and beauty of our Earth Mother.[27]

While Earth Mother teaches acceptance and nourishes us, Sky Father teaches transcendence and liberation, to gain release from harmful relationships, substances, and desires. When pipe smoke is breathed out by exhaling, this calls attention to that which must be released—transcended. The puffs of smoke ascend from Earth to Sky. Drawing on the pipe brings smoke into the mouth and calls attention and realization to that which in life is accepted. Thus, the inhaling and exhaling of the smoke is as the ebb and flow of life.[28]

The Sacred Pipe and what it symbolizes are part of the Native American view of life—that the Source and center of all existence is pure spirit, existing in all created things simultaneously as Great Spirit.[29]

Joseph Epes Brown so powerfully states:

> As the pipe is filled with the sacred tobacco, prayers are offered for all the powers of the universe, and for the myriad forms of creation, each of which is represented by a grain of tobacco. . . . Indeed, in the liberation of the smoke, one is helped not only to find the God's presence within, but also to realize that oneself and the world are mysteriously plunged into God.[30]

Chapter 4

Nick Black Elk once said, "Peace . . . comes within the souls of men when they realize their relationship, their oneness, with the universe and all its powers and when they realize that at the center of the Universe dwells Wakan Tanka, and that this center is really everywhere, it is within each of us."[31]

5

Smoking the Sacred Pipe

The Sacred Pipe is essential for life, because it is with tobacco smoke offered through fire or the medium of the pipe that humans can pray for the necessities of life. For this reason, Francis La Flesche,[1] a researcher writing in the early 1900s, interprets the Osage ritual affirmation, "I am a person who is made of a pipe his body," to mean that the pipe is the "life symbol" of the people. Pipes were given to individuals by these spiritual beings for use by families, clans, societies, and whole tribes. Through the medium of the pipe, people can heal the sick, affect the weather, ask the animals to give themselves to people for food, and make peace.[2]

John Fire Lame Deer explains: "For us Indians there is just the pipe, the earth we sit on, and the open sky. Smoke from the Peace Pipe goes straight up to the spirit world. But this is a two-way thing: Power flows down through that smoke, and through that pipe stem. I feel that power. As I hold my pipe, it moves from the pipe right into my body; it makes my hair stand up. That pipe is not just a thing; it is alive."[3]

The Sacred Pipe helps us stay on the path of the Good Red Road, which can best be described as conducting our lives in a way that puts us in harmony with all of creation. This spiritual path is based on the understanding that we are all part of the great circle of life, and being "spiritual" means finding our place and proper function in this circle. All places in the circle are of equal importance; none is above the others.[4]

The Good Red Road is a nature-based faith. If we separate its ways and ceremonies from nature, all we have left is just another religion. Native spirituality isn't rooted in dogma or under our control.[5]

Each Sacred Pipe has a special "medicine" so it can do its part in restoring us all to the great unity. A personal pipe usually has a more general medicine of being a teacher, protector, and intercessor for the one it dwells with, helping him or her deal with the day-to-day issues of life and restoring the pipe carrier to harmony and balance.[6]

In telling his version of the story of White Buffalo Calf Woman, Archie Lame Deer, a medicine man from South Dakota's Rosebud Reservation, reported that she said: "With this holy pipe you will walk a living prayer. With your feet resting upon the earth and the pipe stem reaching into the sky, your body forms a living bridge between the Sacred Breath and the Sacred Above."[7]

When there is concentration on, attention to, and recognition of this reality while one is smoking the Sacred Pipe, a powerful transformation occurs. "The smoke becomes sacred. The spirit of God in us all becomes visible as sacred smoke."[8]

As Joseph Epes Brown so powerfully states: "The smoke that rises to the heavens is visible prayer for which the entire creation rejoices." It is therefore not without reason that it is commonly called a "peace pipe" and was always used in establishing a relationship, or peace, between friends, but also enemies. In smoking the pipe together, "each person is aided in remembering his or her own center, which is now understood to be the same center of every other person, and of the Universe itself."[9]

John Fire Lame Deer provides a powerful description of smoking the pipe:

> I held the pipe. The bowl was my flesh. The stem stood for all the generations. I felt my blood going into the pipe. I felt it coming back. I feel the pipe coming alive in my hands, felt it move. I felt a power surging from it into my body, filling all of me. Tears were streaming down my face. I knew that within this pipe were

all the powers of nature, that within this pipe was me. I knew that when I smoked the pipe I was the center of all things, giving myself to the Great Spirit.[10]

The Sacred Pipe is a gift of the great Mystery, Wakan Tanka, or Taku Wakan, and it begins with the union of a man and a woman. With the pipe, we give birth, we create, imitating the Great Spirit, action in nature, but in this case we do the action ourselves—by joining bowl with stem. The pipe circle creates a circle of spiritual unity among all the people present. The pipe ceremony is an act of conception, but in this case, one orchestrated by a human person and offered to the Great Mystery, in this way communicating with Him.[11]

That the Sacred Pipe is a force of nature was frequently brought home to me at Sun Bear's apprenticeship program in 1988. Often when he led the pipe ceremony, the wind would pick up on the calmest days. I was told that during one of Sun Bear's pipe ceremonies, a large tree broke in half and came crashing to the ground not far from where the group was sitting.

In one of Sun Bear's advanced pipe programs I attended, Shawnodese, Wabun's partner and coleader, said with chagrin that he was awed by the way the winds kicked up when Sun Bear led a pipe ceremony. But they didn't do that for him. As Shawnodese loaded his pipe, the winds began to blow on what was, up to then, a completely calm day. By the time his pipe was loaded, the wind was so strong he had trouble lighting his pipe.

In one of the later programs, I met a journalist who was one of the participants; he had covered Sun Bear when he took a group of apprentices to Hawaii. Until the journalist saw a powerful scene with his own eyes, he was very skeptical. The group was settled on the beach when Sun Bear began the pipe ceremony. Soon dolphins and small whales moved close to the beach and began beating their tails rhythmically on the surface of the water. The journalist admitted to me that at that point he lost his skepticism.

But sometimes the power of the Sacred Pipe is much more subtle, especially when it involves inner healing. A medicine woman told me of a man she was teaching who had been in psychotherapy for some time before he had taken up the pipe. He prayed the pipe daily, and the therapist was in awe at how quickly he began working through his feelings.

Of course, psychological healing isn't always a pleasant experience. In 1988, I was going through a painful breakup with a woman. I lived on a small farm and had a lot of space to do pipes. During a six-month period, I did a pipe ceremony in the morning and one at sunset. Hoping for some peace of mind, I found instead that the pipe ceremonies intensified painful feelings. But I kept doing daily pipe ceremonies for half a year.

It wasn't until about three months into the daily pipe ceremonies that I began to feel some acceptance and inner peace. As I gained perspective, I realized that the pipe was bringing painful feelings to the surface and intensifying them so they could be released. The process moved me through some very old, buried feelings that I probably couldn't have gotten to except through perhaps psychotherapy—and it would have taken much longer. The pipe was giving me what I *needed*, not what I consciously *wanted*. Often the pipe is much wiser than we are.

Preparing for the Pipe Ceremony

The traditional way to obtain a pipe is by having it gifted to you by a medicine man or woman. However, some people interested in becoming pipe carriers don't live near a reservation or a medicine person or have the time or money to seek someone out on a reservation.

Many non-Natives I have talked to were clearly guided by Spirit to obtain a pipe. A woman who lived near a reservation in northern Wisconsin felt compelled to buy a pipe with an ivory bowl. "I knew it was my pipe," she told me. She took it to an old Lakota medicine man visiting the reservation and asked him to bless it for her. Responding with suspicion, he demanded, "Where did you get this?" She replied, "I was drawn to it. I bought it, and I know it's my pipe." He replied, "I will take it from you and ask Spirit if it is your pipe. If it isn't, I'll keep it. If it is, I will bless it for you and give it back." She immediately agreed, so certain was she that it was her pipe. The next day the medicine man brought it back saying, "It is your pipe. It belongs with you." And that night he took her into his sweat lodge and awakened the pipe for her.

Another woman told me a story that illustrates how everything falls into place when it's time to have a pipe. Prior to attending a program on Native spirituality, the woman had a vision of a pipe that was somehow connected to the eagle. After the vision, she saw eagles woven into jewelry, eagles flying overhead—eagles everywhere. But when she got to the program, she found that the other participants had bought all the pipes available. For her pipe, she was directed to go to the pipe maker who lived on the mountain where the program was being held. When she arrived, he had only *one* pipe left—with a bowl carved into the shape of an eagle!

Conversely, many years ago I met a man at a weekend conference where I was doing a pipe ceremony and sweat lodge. As I was walking to my truck at the end of the conference, he stopped me and told me his story: In the late 1960s, he and some friends were hitchhiking and taking buses around the Southwest. While they were visiting a reservation, a medicine man gave him a pipe. He had no idea what to do with it and later smoked pot in it with his friends. Possibly because he was feeling guilty, he left the pipe on the bus when he left to hitchhike on his own. Three days later, a truck driver dropped him at the on-ramp to a town where he intended to spend the night. When he turned around, he saw the pipe sitting on the curb! A long time later he told the story to a medicine man during a sweat lodge, and the man grabbed him and exclaimed, "You didn't lose that pipe, that pipe lost you!"

Since the man still didn't know much about the pipe, I gave him some material to read, some tobacco, and my phone number. I said that if he was still interested after he read what I gave him, I would send him more material and talk to him about the pipe. He never called.

I acquired my pipe in 1987 after having dropped out of organized religion seventeen years earlier. Seized by an impulse to "get some religion," I drove to Madison, Wisconsin, expecting to buy my usual fare of books: Christian mysticism, Hinduism, and Buddhism. Instead, I bought only books on Native American spirituality. Before I returned home, a friend asked to borrow the only book that wasn't Native American—one on "channeling" I'd bought on a lark.

The books sat on my shelf for three months, until one day I pulled one out and started reading. After reading about thirty pages, none of which mentioned the pipe, I felt I *had* to get a pipe. A month later, I drove to Grand Portage, Minnesota, with a couple of friends to attend an art therapy conference with a Native American theme. After a presentation by a young medicine man, I told him about my recent interest and asked if my next step was to buy a pipe. Though in his thirties, he was very traditional and exclaimed, "Absolutely not! That would take you down the road to destruction."

The next day while browsing at the lodge's gift shop, I looked at the one pipe they had in their display case. Its price tag said $120—too expensive for me in 1987. But on the last day of the conference, I returned to the gift shop with a friend and noticed that the pipe was now eighty dollars. When I asked the clerk, she said that it had always been eighty dollars (not true, but I certainly wasn't going to argue). Telling my friend how the medicine man had warned me not to buy a pipe, I reached in my pocket for my credit card. My friend said, "You just said that buying a pipe was the road to destruction." Smiling, I agreed as I handed the clerk my credit card. At that point, there seemed to be two of me: one (my mind) that accepted the medicine man's injunction, and the other (my soul) that seemed to be buying the pipe for me.

I was certain the pipe was mine, and I remember cradling it in the crook of my arm during the long drive home. A couple of months later, I attended a workshop outside of Madison where a man, part Apache and a Medi Pipe Carrier, was to do a sweat lodge. I asked him if he would bless my pipe and he reluctantly told me to bring a tobacco offering for him and we would talk about it. That's when things suddenly started to open up. When I asked a woman conference participant for couple of cigarettes to crush up for tobacco, she asked me what it was for. When I told her, she responded, "Find Randy." Randy was a pipe smoker. Randy, it turned out, had sage he had collected from Bear Butte, in South Dakota, and he gifted it to me along with a pouch full of tobacco.

The medicine man agreed to put my pipe on the altar outside the sweat lodge and ask Spirit if he could bless it. At the end of the first round of the lodge, he brought the pipe in and blessed it. After the sweat lodge, he stayed inside with me after the other participants left, telling me that it was my pipe and that I should explore the symbolism in the bowl and stem.

Before returning home, I swung past Madison and visited the friend who'd borrowed my channeling book. After two near-death experiences earlier in her life, she was frequently visited by a Hindu holy man in her meditations. A famous guru, Baba Muktananda, told her that her holy man was in fact a famous Hindu master from many decades past.

I asked her to ask her holy man about my pipe. Holding the pipe and channeling her holy man, she told me that the pipe maker was not around Grand Portage, Minnesota, where I bought the pipe, but lived in a town with "valley" in its name. But summers he made pipes at a place called "Pipestone." Neither she nor I knew where that was. She said that if I went there, I would find him, adding, "It's your pipe. He made it for you. He doesn't know your face, but he knows your soul. When you hand it to him, he will tell you that it's like meeting with an old friend." She said that he was in Minneapolis when he made the pipe and a female friend had asked to take some of his pipes with her on her trip through Grand Portage.

I found out about *Pipestone National Monument* and called and asked about the pipe maker who had inscribed the bottom of my pipe with his medicine name. They knew him well and sent some newspaper articles, one with a picture of him working on a pipe in what looked like a garage. I wrote the pipe maker but he didn't answer. Undaunted, I drove all the way to *Pipestone*, but he wasn't there. I was told that he was staying in the hotel in the "village"—an area with a grocery store, gas station, and hotel. At the hotel, the manager saw his car, but his room was locked. When asked if there was a garage, he took me to it. My pipe maker was just firing the outside of a stem. He told me that he had gotten my letter and that he would be finished in a minute.

He then took me to his hotel room and we talked. When I handed him the pipe, he cradled it in his arms and said, "I feel like I'm meeting an old friend," and he remembered when and where he had made the pipe. He confirmed that he lived in Brown *Valley*, but was in Minneapolis when he made the pipe. A female friend asked to take some of his pipes on a trip she was taking through Grand Portage. Though he seemed shy at first, we talked for about five hours; and he shared personal things about his life and some of his secret powers.

Because it was a hot day, I had food in the car and no place to stay that night (in the middle of Memorial Day weekend), and I was about ten hours from my home, I had to leave. But it felt as if he would have been willing to talk to me all night. Elated, I called my "channeling" friend in Madison and told her that the visit had unfolded exactly as she said it would. But nothing came up about his "not knowing my face, but knowing my soul." She exclaimed, "You're a white 'honky' from Wisconsin who he didn't know from Adam, but he had an intimate talk with you for hours. You don't think he knows your soul?" I'm not quite as dense now as I was back then.

AWAKENING THE PIPE

A pipe is simply a chunk of stone and a piece of wood, and nothing else. However, when the pipe is *awakened* by a medicine man or woman, it becomes a Sacred Pipe filled with power of its own. When the pipe is blessed (consecrated) and bound to the prospective pipe carrier, it becomes a Sacred Pipe.

The awakening ceremony differs among the various traditions. When my first pipe was blessed in 1987, it was set on the altar outside a sweat lodge conducted by a man who was part Apache. When he got permission, he brought my pipe in and blessed it, circling it over the steam from the heated stones he had sprinkled with sage and sweetgrass.

A year later when I began Sun Bear's apprentice program on a mountain outside Spokane, I stood in line to have my pipe blessed in Sun Bear's tradition. The people ahead of me in line had bought their pipes that day, whereas I had been smoking mine for a year. With each person before me, the Ojibwa medicine woman blessing the pipes told the individual to smoke the pipe for six months before doing a group ceremony with it.

In the ceremony she did with me, the medicine woman smudged the pipe and then joined bowl and stem as I sat opposite her. She handed me the pipe, which I held palms upward in front of me. She placed her hands over mine, touching my wrists with her fingertips at the pulse points. She had me repeat an oath committing myself to the way of the pipe—a path of service. After several moments of meditation with her eyes closed, she signaled that she was finished. Before I got up, she told me to smoke my pipe alone for three months—not six—before I did a pipe with a group, because I was already bonded with it. I was pleased that even my smoking without instruction had helped in the bonding.

A number of years later, when I was trained and empowered to bless and bind pipes, I learned that she had reached into my solar plexus and pulled tendrils of energy—sort of light filaments—and wrapped them around the pipe and my hands, binding me with the Sacred Pipe.

When I was taught to bless and bind pipes by Sun Bear, Waban, and Shawnodese in an advanced group in the early 1990s, I wondered how I would "know," as I passed the pipe over the burning sage, when it was awakened. Both teachers shared how they got subtle hints when a pipe was awakened. One said she saw colors; the other felt a tug in his solar plexus. Back in those days I didn't feel I was attuned to subtle energies.

Eventually, I awakened my first pipe. I closed my eyes and intently concentrated on the process as I passed the bowl over the burning sage, desperately hoping I would be able to tell when the pipe was awakened. I was shocked when the bowl began to pulsate in my hand as if I were holding a beating human heart. I was so surprised I almost dropped the bowl, but I maintained my composure. Fortunately, the new pipe carrier had his eyes closed.

From my very first attempt, I received a clear physical indication when the pipe was awakening. And, since then, each time I awaken a pipe, it feels like a new experience—and I still feel the pulsating.

Yet when a Lakota holy man from Rapid City, South Dakota, blessed my group pipe, he laid it on a table, fanned smudge smoke on it with a feathered fan, and chanted for some time. Each tradition has its own way of awakening and blessing a pipe.

When people's pipes are awakened and they begin to smoke them, the experience seems to reverberate and ripple through their lives. Initially, pipe carriers get a great deal of help and guidance to move them on their spiritual path—often by natural signs and people showing up at just the right time. At first, things begin to flow more easily. Of course, when they evolve to a certain point, they are "tested," eventually "get it," and then move on to their next lessons—as is true in many spiritual traditions.

The impact that an awakened pipe can have on an individual was somewhat humorously brought home to me when I awakened a pipe for a nurse who was in the same shamanic training I was in. She had read everything I'd given her and was really committed to the Path of the Pipe. When I was awakening her pipe, I shared with her a strong image I was having of a bear—suggesting that the bear totem was strong with her, or with the pipe. That night she called her husband and learned that a bear was camping out in her backyard. (Their house was on the outer edge of a suburb!) And when she returned home, there were eight bears in her backyard, and they didn't leave until mating season.

When a pipe is awakened, the Sacred Pipe becomes a powerful tool that must be treated with respect. Wallace Black Elk likens the Sacred Pipe to "a radio, like radar. You communicate from here directly to that main Chanunpa [Sacred Pipe]. You could communicate directly with the wisdom."[12] Medicine woman Evelyn Eaton states that "the function of the pipe [is] to be the two-way communication, the 'pipeline' between the Great Spirit and His children."[13]

Virtually all earth-centered practitioners have some physical object of the earth that is used for ceremonial purposes. And the pipe becomes a focus for communion with the spirit world and an honoring of the soul and spirit essence in all creation. It's a tool for balancing between the worlds and developing depth of spirit for those on the earth-path. Each part of the pipe ceremony represents communion with a sacred arche-type of the universe: a spirit being, a star, a circle, a tree—representing the Tree of Life. The pipe ceremony is filled with the directed intention of Spirit, focusing on the act of uniting Heaven, Earth, and humankind.[14]

The pipe catapults the pipe carrier and participants beyond everyday reality into an awareness and understanding of deeper sacred truths. And when bowl and stem are united, the inherent duality of the universe is made one.[15]

Jim Tree reminds us that the awakened pipe is more than just a pow-erful instrument for ceremony to access the attention of the Divine. The Sacred Pipe is intended to become the residence of a beneficial spirit, who comes to us to teach, guide, protect, nurture, provide, and intercede for us.[16] The spirit that dwells in the pipe after it is awakened is a living guide (such as a power animal, ancestor, spirit, or angel—whatever form a particular individual can personally accept and relate to).[17] And the spirit knows the way to harmony and can lead us to the destination.[18]

My sense is that a spirit or spirits move toward the pipe when it is being awakened. At that point, an individual spirit specifically appropri-ate for the pipe and the prospective pipe carrier moves into the pipe and the pipe becomes awakened—alive with the spirit. And as Jim Tree states, "The pipe is a divine gift to us and it works, not because we have faith it will, but because it is a real, living entity that takes action independent of us, or if we are fortunate, interdependent with us."[19]

STORING THE PIPE

In the pipe bag, we need the essentials: pouch of smoking mix, tamper, various medicine objects, and herbs such as sage, cedar, and sweetgrass. Bear Root is an herb that is known to help protect the Sacred Pipe from things that could interfere with its medicine. The pipe needs to be wrapped—with the bowl in a piece of leather or cloth to be separate from the stem and the other objects. Working with a Lakota, I was taught to wrap the bowl and stem separately in red felt cloths, putting sage around them for protection.

Sundance sage (longleaf sage) can be tied to the stem, as a way of protecting it. The idea of wrapping the stem and bowl separately is not only to cushion the objects in the bag, but also to keep them covered from view until they are about to be used.[20]

The proper way to hold a pipe, whether assembled or in the bag, is in the crook of the left arm, the one closest to our heart.

PERFORMING THE PIPE CEREMONY

First, we must find an area where we would like to smoke the Sacred Pipe.

Smudging

It is appropriate to burn some flat cedar to make the area clear of any negativity. Cedar repels "bugs" not only in the physical world, but also in the spiritual. One could also burn sweetgrass to invite in positive energies. It is useful to have sweetgrass burning continually while filling the pipe, but sweetgrass is hard to keep burning.[21]

We should never blow on any kind of burning smudge, but rather fan it with our hand or a feather, or simply wave it back and forth, to keep it burning. Some people say that it is disrespectful to the spirit of the herb to blow forcefully on the smudge.[22]

Pipe carriers purify themselves before touching the pipe. Smudging is an act of "washing" themselves and the participants of the pipe circle with a burning herb—not only cedar, but usually sage, and some people use wormwood.[23] The dried herb is placed in a bowl, usually a shell from the sea, for example an abalone shell, and the herb is ignited. The flame is then extinguished, allowing the herb to smolder, producing a purifying smoke.

There are many ways to smudge, but pipe carriers often pass their hands over the burning sage and then fan smoke over their body with cupped palms, bringing it to their solar plexus, heart, and head. The bowl as usually passed over the smudge first. In most traditions, pipe carriers face east. They pass bowl over the smudge, first scooping it toward the east; then, turning bowl around, moving it from west to east; then from south to north, and north to south. And once the bowl is smudged, the two ends containing the holes can be smudged. We can also make circles with the bowl over the smudge, first on one side then the other.

The stem is smudged the same way. Then when the stem is smudged, the holes on the ends of the stem are circled over the smudge. Then the implements, which are usually cleansed last, are passed over the smudge.

The act of smudging demarcates the ceremony in time, signaling that from this point on, what is done is in the timelessness of the sacred. The pipe carrier's mind has a chance to quiet itself, and the participants take on the proper attitude and state of mind. The smudging signals that what is to follow is a sacred act, set off from what has gone before.[24]

Asking Permission

Pipe carriers can wet the *tang* of the pipe (the end of the stem that fits into the bowl) with their mouths in order to swell the wood and provide for a good fit and seal.

Before the pipe is loaded, it is traditional to request permission from the Great Spirit to smoke the Sacred Pipe. If permission isn't granted, we should move to a different spot. I heard about a guy who smoked in the spot even though he didn't feel he had permission and it didn't "feel" right. He got poison ivy. Another heeded the warning and found an area a short distance from the tree he was originally standing under, only to have a huge limb break off and crash down on the place he had vacated.

In asking permission, pipe carriers can hold the bowl in the left hand and stem in the right—separated by a few inches—with arms raised above the head. When it feels as if permission is granted, they join the two parts of the Sacred Pipe together—wedding the male stem and female bowl—representing the two aspects of the Creator: Father Sky and Mother Earth.

The bowl and stem are joined and, at that timeless moment of unity, the duality of the universe dissolves. This act is central to the nature and purpose of the pipe: through the joining and the participatory smoking of the pipe, divisions—between human and nonhuman, between people and cultures, between secular and sacred—are transcended, and all things become one.[25]

When the parts are wedded together, the Sacred Pipe becomes a loaded gun—a tool for concentrating spiritual energy. The pipe carrier then may request protection while smoking and ask for health and help.

Filling the Pipe

Once everything is smudged, pipe carriers continue to face east, beginning the ceremony proper by filling the pipe. There are many different ways to hold or position the pipe, depending on the tribal tradition. In Jim Tree's tradition, pipe carriers hold the pipe bowl in the left hand, with the stem either over the left shoulder or in the crook of the left arm. Pinches of tobacco are then placed into the bowl with the right hand.[26]

I was taught two ceremonies and use both, depending on the situation. The first involves sitting on the ground and filling the pipe that is held in the crook of the left arm, with stem resting on the shoulder, left hand holding the bowl. The second ceremony is much more dramatic and visual. Pipe carriers hold the pipe bowl in the left hand, with stem pointing outward and upward, while filling the pipe. This ceremony is more visual and effective for a very large group—one that is far too big to sit in a circle.

In some traditions, a song is sung during the filling of the pipe; in others, there is no song, or a song is sung only at the end of the ceremony.

It's not the size of the tobacco offering but the intent that matters. And when offering prayers, it may be easier for some pipe carriers to offer tobacco to the spirits when they are thought of as physical ancestors or elders.[27]

The smoking mix is a physical representation of our spiritual intentions, held out to the forces of the universe to continually remind them of our request or prayers. We put out an energetic impulse—like electricity—through a thought generated by our brain.[28] We set our intent and the tobacco holds the energy and, when burned, sends the message in the form of smoke up to the Heavens.

While facing east (in most traditions), pipe carriers offer each pinch of the sacred smoking mixture to Father Sky, Mother Earth, and the Powers of the Four Cardinal Directions before placing it in the bowl. Then they extend their hand to the east and call in the Spirit Keeper of the East. Then extending their hand to their right, to the south, they call in the Spirit Keeper of the South. They can then reach over their head, extending their arm to the back of them for the west, calling in the Spirit Keeper that represents that direction, and then reaching to their left, call in the Spirit Keeper of the North.

After calling in the Spirit Keepers of each direction, the pipe carrier continues to fill the pipe, offering each pinch to the Sky, Earth, and the Four Directions, beginning in the east.

A pinch of tobacco is offered to the Four Directions three more times—completing the first round of four pinches.

For the remaining three rounds, any multiple of four can be used—perhaps for the four races of humankind: yellow, red, black, and white; for the elementals: earth, air fire, and water; for healing: mental, emotional, spiritual, and physical; for the four kingdoms: plant, animal, mineral, human; for the animal kingdom: creepy-crawlies, swimmers, flyers, and four-leggeds; for the plant kingdom: the mosses, flowering things, bushes, and trees; for basic human virtues: faith, hope, wisdom, and strength; for the emotional states: joy, peace, love, and trust; for the world: peace, an end to world hunger, healing of the earth, and planetary enlightenment. Any four characteristics.

With each pinch, pipe carriers may utter an invocation, such as:

> *Creator, Mother Earth, all our relations,*
> *all the spirits of this place,*
> *in the spirit of all the pipe ceremonies*
> *that have come before us,*
> *I ask you to come in and join us now.*
> *There is a place for you in this Pipe.*

A similar prayer can be invoked when inviting in the elementals, and the plant, mineral, animal, and human kingdoms. For example:

> *I call on the Powers of the Four Directions,*
> *the stone people,*
> *all the star nations,*
> *all who have walked this path before us,*
> *I invite you to join us now.*
> *There is a place for you in this Pipe.*

Depending on the size of the pipe bowl and/or whether it is to be shared with a pipe circle, the tobacco pinches are offered in multiples of four until the bowl is filled. If a larger pipe load is desired because, for example, it is to be a group pipe, more pinches may be offered—always a multiple of four (four, eight, twelve pinches).

There is an art to filling a pipe bowl. Each pinch of tobacco should be put in carefully so it drops all the way to the bottom; tamp down *lightly* to make sure that it fills the bottom of the bowl. Continue to fill the pipe, making sure the tobacco is distributed uniformly. If the pipe is filled too loosely, there will be air pockets in the tobacco and it will burn fast or not support the fire for long. If it is filled too tightly, it may be impossible to draw air through the stem. Filled optimally, it will burn steadily and be less apt to go out.

When the Sacred Pipe is filled, it is usually smoked immediately by the pipe carrier or shared with a pipe circle. However, if it is a group ceremony, for example a sweat lodge, a plug of sage leaves made by rolling the sage into a ball can be placed in the top of the bowl so that the contents are protected by the spirit of the sage until it is used during the ceremony.

Smoking the Pipe

Once filled, the pipe is lit. Sometimes pipes want to be lit only by a piece of coal or a lightning-struck stick. Some don't want to be lit with a butane lighter.[29] Many pipe carriers use a book or, better yet, a small box of wooden kitchen matches. They strike easily and a person can hold the bowl in the left hand and still hold the box—striking edge out—with that hand while striking with the right.

In the process of smoking the pipe, people engage in a deeply inter-active process with the Creator, indeed with all the realms of nature, spirit, and the cosmos. As we draw on the pipe, our breath blends with the sacred smoke inside our body. Thus, a portion of this sacred prayer remains in the body for a moment so that the body mingles with the prayer. With each puff, the prayer, in the form of smoke, leaves the body and rises up to the Creator, becoming a part of the universe—and the person becomes joined with all things.[30]

With our intention, the physical (herbs) is transformed into spiritual (energy) by fire, and the thoughts are carried up and dispersed into the whole cosmos and come to the attention of the Creator.

Some people teach to vary the ceremony so that it doesn't become routine. I think with pipe carriers who have a number of teachers and are exposed to a number of traditions, this makes sense. But I choose to stick to the two primary ceremonies I learned and received permission to use. For me, being a non-Native, when a ceremony is done with attention and care down through the ages, it gathers power within itself. Also, by doing it in the way I was taught, I honor my teachers.

As soon as the Sacred Pipe is lit, a puff of smoke is offered to the Sky, Earth, and the Four Directions. It may also be offered to the spirits of those who dwell in the place where we are smoking and to all who have smoked the Sacred Pipe down through the ages.

In some ceremonies, pipe carriers sit on the ground and blow a puff of smoke to Father Sky and Mother Earth and the Four Directions. Without moving, they twist their bodies around to blow smoke in each of the directions.

Some ceremonies involve pipe carriers standing, facing east, and extending their arm, pointing to the sky with the stem, as they send a puff to Father Sky—inviting Him to smoke the pipe with them; then to the Earth, sending a puff to Mother Earth, perhaps touching the ground with the tip of the stem, inviting Her to smoke the pipe. Still facing east, they point the stem to the sacred East, take another draw on the pipe, and blow a puff in that direction. Then they "pivot" their bodies to their right and, while pointing the pipe stem to the South, blow a puff in that direction. They continue to rotate their bodies clockwise for the West and North, drawing smoke from the pipe, pointing the stem and blowing the smoke in each direction. Completing the rotation, they return to the East.

The standing position seems to work well when a person is doing a pipe alone. The movements seem to enhance concentration and intent. It is also a good ceremony—because it is so visual—to do before a very large group. If the pipe carrier is in a pipe circle, of course, the sitting position is preferable because it makes the pipe carrier a link in an unbroken circle and not disconnected from the group.

Then the pipe stem may be pointed skyward above the head, sometimes with the bowl against the heart, and a prayer may be sent through Grandfather and Grandmother Eagle to the Great Spirit, beseeching sacred Eagle to "send a voice to the Creator that all my people may live." "People," of course, meaning "all living things." While holding the pipe above the head with stem pointing skyward, the pipe carrier may offer a simple prayer or request of a few words. But the initial prayer should be kept short. (Too long, and the pipe might go out.)

In some traditions, people are not to take any smoke into their lungs; they just mix it in their mouth. Then the offering is blown out to the Creator. In other traditions, some of the smoke is taken into the lungs to mingle with the body before blowing it to the Heavens. The smoke isn't for the smoker, but for the Great Spirit.

In a group ceremony—a pipe circle—participants pass the pipe in a clockwise direction, accepting the pipe bowl with the left hand (their receptive hand; the one closest to the heart) and the stem with the right (the active, giving side). The pipe is offered to the person on their left and it is handed over in such a way that others can receive the bowl with their left hand and stem with their right. When receiving the pipe, participants rotate the stem around to their mouth in a clockwise direction, thus completing the circle started by the one who handed it to them. Participants should hold the pipe by the bowl at all times, preventing the bowl from falling off the stem.[31] A tamper and matches can be passed around the circle in case the pipe goes out before it is returned to the one conducting the ceremony. (Some participants have their own matches and tamper ready to facilitate the ceremony.) Once the pipe has gone around the circle, the leader smokes all of the smoking mixture that is left.

When participants receive the pipe, they should remain faithful to the structure of the ceremony—doing what the person conducting the ceremony has led them to do. I have attended ceremonies where a participant may do an elaborate personal ritual, moving the pipe around in complicated ways and even chanting before giving it to the person on their left. This seems to be annoying to other participants, as the person seems to go off in their own little world, disconnecting from other participants. It's probable that other participants have been to pipe ceremonies and know a variety of rituals, too. It seems somewhat pretentious, if not disrespectful to the leader and other participants, to briefly conduct their own ceremony. It breaks the uniformity of the ritual and interrupts the flow of passing the pipe.

While smoking, participants should keep their mouth right next to the pipe stem at all times. If there is too much time between puffs, the fire can go out. If the participant isn't getting much smoke but the tobacco is still lit, the tobacco should be tapped down to fill any air pockets that have formed and/or the thumb placed over the hole in the bowl, opening and closing it. Using the thumb as a damper sometime coaxes the fire to intensify.

Upon completing the ceremony, some pipe carriers place the tip of the pipe bowl to the earth with the stem pointing east at a forty-five-degree angle to the sky. Then as they disconnect the stem from the bowl, they may speak to the spirits who have gathered, telling them how grateful they are they that they joined them. Or pipe carriers can raise the joined pipe above their head, thanking the Creator for the privilege of smoking the pipe, before disconnecting bowl and stem. Pipe carriers might then send the guardian spirits that showed up for the ceremony "home" with their blessings. It's important to be polite, respectful, and thankful to the spirits.[32]

The ashes from the pipe are mixed with those of the herbs used in smudging and then given back to Mother Earth. Spilled mix also. In the event that none is spilled, a pinch from the pouch can be offered.[33] Then the pipe is cleaned.

Some pipe carriers end the ceremony by smudging everything again with sage, letting the smoke enter the holes of the bowl and stem. Then the bowl can be plugged with sage if needed. This will keep the "council lodge" (the bowl) clean and ready for the next "gathering." Everything is then wrapped, placed carefully back into the pipe bag, and kept in a safe place until the next ceremony.[34]

Cleaning the Pipe

After taking the pipe apart, before putting it away, pipe carriers should run a cleansing rod through the stem while the resins are still warm and wet. A metal coat hanger can work for this. Each time the rod is pushed through, its end can be cleaned off with a rag, before it is pulled out. Then push it through again, cleaning the end of the rod protruding beyond the stem—continuing the procedure until the stem seems is clear. Running a large guitar string or small bass string through the stem helps clean it if it's not plugged. Sometimes it may be necessary to heat a smudged rod so it is red hot, and then pass it through the stem to clean out anything that is plugging it. If it isn't clean for the next ceremony, participants might not be able to bring air through it.

Since most stems are two pieces of wood glued together, hot water may adversely affect the stem. But once the stem is clean, the "sacred" coat hanger rod can be put back in the stem before it is put away. It is useful to bend the end of the coat hanger into a circle or oval, providing a "handle" for removing it. Some pipe carriers hang feathers on the "handle" for aesthetic purposes.

The bowl can be cleaned by tapping it against one's hand or, if necessary, by digging out anything that is stuck inside with the end of the hanger. If the bowl becomes plugged, a commercial (metal) pipe "spoon" can be used to dig out anything that is still stuck. Since pipestone is soft, care must be taken to dig out the tobacco in such a way that the bowl isn't scratched inside.

Periodically, the bowl can be cleaned thoroughly with a nipple brush with warm, soapy water—poking it into each of the two holes (top and bottom), twisting and turning it until it is clean. After rinsing, the bowl can then be carefully placed upside down so that water can drip out and it can dry quickly. If a bowl loses its sheen, the outside can be covered with beeswax and placed in an oven at low heat until the wax melts.

Jim Tree says that if he is taking the pipe out of its bundle to clean it, he always smudges it and offers some tobacco or mix to its spirit. He explains to the pipe that he is cleaning it and the pipe seems to "relax."[35]

SPECIAL CONSIDERATIONS AND WARNINGS

Occasionally people buy old pipes in trading posts or Native American stores—pipes that have been awakened and used by someone else. What does a pipe carrier do if he or she obtains such a pipe? Elders tell people sometimes to bury the pipe for months—giving it back to the earth and letting the earth cleanse it. Sometimes an awakened pipe can be brought into a sweat lodge for cleansing, but it may take many times.[36]

One elder shared with me that sometimes abandoned or sold pipes are angry and have to be thoroughly cleansed or even buried forever. I once found a very old pipe stem I really liked at a trading post. But the Native woman there said it couldn't be sold separately. They were a "set." Interestingly, the stem didn't seem to even belong to the bowl and was a poor fit. But she said mysteriously, "This is your pipe. You are supposed to have it." (In a later contact I had with her, she proved to be very connected to Spirit.)

I bought the pipe and was told by a spiritual teacher that it was angry. The pipe had belonged to a Native man who had lost his leg. He had died but didn't yet realize he was dead, and some of his angry energy was still on the bowl. I was told to bury it for four months, and I did.

I wasn't sure why I was supposed to have the pipe, but sensed I was. The end of the four-month time period coincided with a week's vacation I was planning at Devil's Lake, north of Madison, Wisconsin. After arranging for a cabin, I drove into the park, and walking toward the shelter house, I ruminated about a feeling I had been having for several days: I felt guided to do pipe ceremonies at Devil's Lake, perhaps to reactivate the site. Prior to whites taking over, Native Americans had lived around what they called "Spirit Lake" for many years.

At the time I felt that the idea seemed pretentious. I didn't have a drop of Native blood in me. I guess I was subconsciously asking for a sign. As I was deep in thought, a turkey vulture circled just above my head three times. On the fourth pass, it must have hit an air pocket, because it dropped slightly, beat its wings vigorously until it righted itself, and flew off. I said out loud, "No you don't. If I'm supposed to do pipes, I need a fourth pass." Though the bird was about seventy-five yards away, it abruptly turned around, flew just above my head, and made a perfect fourth circle.

During my week-long vacation, I smoked multiple pipes in each of the directions, mostly on the surrounding cliffs, and had some powerful experiences during the ceremonies. Once, while smoking on a cliff far away from any turkey vultures, I had about twenty-five circling just above my head by the time the ceremony was about to end. Walking along the cliff after the last pipe, a woman I was with said, "Look way over there. See all the turkey vultures circling? That means you did good?" I replied, "Not necessarily. Turkey vultures often circle above high cliffs." At her suggestion, we walked over and stood just below them, watching them glide in lazy circles in the sky. Though all of them were circling clockwise, one broke rank, reversed its direction, and began a circle counterclockwise. As it flew past one of the other turkey vultures, they slapped wings—a kind of turkey vulture high five. "Is that *normal*?" my friend asked. "Only at an NBA game," I replied.

At Devil's Lake, I used two pipes—my first pipe, which I had awakened in 1987, and the old pipe I bought at the trading post, with the bowl I had buried. Interestingly, when I returned to the cabin after the very last pipe ceremonies, the old pipe bowl I had bought—because I wanted the stem—somehow burrowed through its wrappings and fell to the ground. Even though the earth was soft, it broke in half.

Surprisingly, I had a clear sense that it had done its job and wasn't to be smoked again. When I got home, I buried it for good. Since my original stem for my first pipe seemed worn out and tasted sour, I had bought the old pipe for the stem. When I did my first pipe ceremony after Devil's Lake, I used the newly purchased stem and the bowl to the pipe I'd bought in 1987; I raised them above my head and asked permission to smoke the pipe. I got a clear "yes," and when I connected bowl and stem, they fit together perfectly. That experience was in 1989 and I still use my original bowl and old stem as my personal pipe.

Buying a New Pipe

Several years later, a friend showed a strong interest in the Sacred Pipe. I had given him material to read, and he later asked for more. Though I wasn't particularly guided to buy him a pipe, his interest was so strong it was clear that it was only a matter of time before he would be ready to have a pipe.

On a visit to Parson's Trading Post in Lake Dalton, Wisconsin, I saw a big, beautiful "Sioux Warrior Pipe." It was a T-style pipe with a large arrowhead extending beyond the bowl. It would have been too expensive for me to buy for myself, but I was willing to spend the money on him.

When I got home, I stored the pipe and waited for the right time to offer it to him. For no apparent reason, he quit talking about the pipe and discontinued interest in it. A couple of years later, I gave up on him and decided to use it as a group pipe, keeping the original pipe I bought exclusively as a personal pipe. (The larger pipe with a much larger bowl has proved to be an excellent group pipe, one I would have passed up if I hadn't thought I was buying it for someone else. Maybe that was the only way I was able to acquire the group pipe I needed.)

Around this time, I had some vacation time but couldn't afford to fly to mountains. I decided to drive to the Black Hills and later see Mount Rushmore. As the vacation date approached, I had the feeling that I should smoke my pipe around sacred sites in South Dakota. Despite strong guidance, I continued to wonder if I was just making it up.

Then synchronicities began to occur. At the end of my run along a river where I jogged daily, I turned to go back and had a clear sense that I was supposed to put three feathers on my pipe. As I was ruminating about it, a Red-tailed Hawk flew above my head and circled three times.

After returning to my office building and cleaning up, I went to the reception area and checked my mailbox for messages before I met with my first afternoon client. In my box was a large envelope with a short leather strip threaded through a large, wooden bead. Sticking in the bead were three Red-tailed Hawk feathers. When I asked a colleague about it, she said that her husband was in the woods and found the feathers, immediately thinking that I should have them. It was a surprise to me since I didn't even know him very well. (After the wolf, the Red-tailed Hawk was the second power animal that came to me, several years earlier.)

The experience of the three feathers triggered a forgotten memory. Many years earlier, during Sun Bear's program, one of his advanced apprentices was excited about decorating her pipe stem. Since I was just starting out, I said, "I thought you weren't supposed to decorate a pipe—it was an insult to the pipe maker." She replied, "That's right, unless you are guided by Spirit." I remember mumbling, "I don't do Spirit; I'm a Capricorn."

After the experience with the gift from my friend's husband, I felt strongly that I should put a strip of wolf fur on my stem, also—to honor the wolf when I smoked the pipe. A short time later, on impulse, I drove to Lake Dalton on my way back home from Madison. The Native woman I had seen only once before—despite many visits to the trading post—was behind the counter. I showed her the pipe I wanted to put a strip of wolf fur on. She was shocked until I told her I had smudged myself before I did a pipe ceremony, just before coming to the shop.

I asked her where I might be able to find wolf skin. She told me of a place in northern Minnesota many miles off the main road I'd be traveling for my upcoming trip to South Dakota. Disappointed, I thanked her and began to leave. She asked, "How much do you need?" I said, "Only a thin strip to wrap around my pipe stem." She said, "Just a minute" and left the store. Since she was the only one in the old part of the store, I was surprised she walked out. Minutes later she returned. Evidently she lived right next door. She handed me a thin strip of gray wolf fur and asked, "Will this work?" I thanked her profusely; it was perfect. But she refused to take money for it.

But the coincidences that occurred helped me understand what it meant to be "guided" by Spirit when it was time to decorate a pipe. And with so many synchronicities, I decided to take the warrior pipe I had bought a long time before with me on the trip. It was clear my friend wouldn't ever come around. But the pipe hadn't been blessed. While attending Wellness Week, an annual health promotion national conference in Stevens Point, Wisconsin, I "just happened" to talk to a participant who said she worked with a holy man in South Dakota. With no address, only a phone number, I called him when I arrived in Rapid City. He agreed to meet with me, and after a lengthy visit, I asked him to bless the warrior pipe. He agreed, and I then had two pipes to smoke at sacred sites.

I got as far west as Devil's Tower, where I smoked the first pipe. Returning then to Mount Rushmore, I approached the State Park. Ahead of me a large Red-tailed Hawk sat perched on a tree just outside the park. It flew ahead of me as if to guide me into the park. Though I remembered it, I didn't think about it again until I finished smoking several pipes in the park and was leaving. On a tree next to the exit sat a Red-tailed Hawk, who looked at me and then flew ahead of me as I left the park.

Before returning home, I did my last pipes at the Wounded Knee Cemetery. As I detached my second pipe and laid it on the felt—to wrap along with the other pipe—a young man who had been selling dream catchers strolled over to me and silently admired my pipes. After wrapping them and putting them in the pipe bags, I said, "I'll bet you don't see a lot of whites smoking pipes here." Thoughtfully, he said, "A few." I was surprised, but pleased that I was one of others who had done the journey.

Though I have now been a pipe carrier for twenty-five years, these experiences from years ago are still with me. Being non-Native, I felt it pretentious to think I was supposed to smoke pipes at sacred sites. That feeling is sort of reverse ego: "Maybe I'm not worthy." Doing things we are guided to do isn't about being "worthy." It doesn't make us "special." We just happened to be in the right place at the right time, and something needs to be done. We're "handy."

But we need to be grateful for the opportunity to be of service, because that's what being a pipe carrier is all about.

Using the Pipe Properly

If we plan to do a pipe, we should abstain from alcohol for several days beforehand. Menstruating women should not participate in pipe ceremonies or even touch a pipe—unless it is their own personal pipe. The exception to that might be an all-women circle where the menstruating woman might bolster the energy of the experience. In a mixed circle, however, woman "on her moon" can overpower the pipe—and the men— in the circle because she is at the height of her personal power. She is in the process of renewing her power to create life. In the old days, it wasn't unusual for a chief to bring two menstruating women to sit on either side of him at a meeting with another chief. The first chief felt women's power gave him an advantage in negotiations.

An awakened pipe should never be brought out just for display or even shown to someone unless the person has positive intent and has been smudged thoroughly. To do so opens it up to the energies of those around it. It would be like taking a newborn baby into a crowded store.[37]

And we shouldn't remove the pipe from its wrappings unless we intend to do ceremony with it. To do so not only invites attention to it from possible unwanted persons or energies, but it also "teases" the spirits. When we put a Sacred Pipe together, we start a chain of events that can't be stopped, regardless of whether we do the rest of the ceremony or not. The ceremony has been designed to give a constructive channel or direction for the power set in motion by connecting pipe and bowl.[38]

Once a pipe is awakened and smoked in a ceremony, it is the home, the body, of a spiritual being, and is considered alive and sacred. Such a pipe should never be sold. If you run across an awakened pipe, it is best to buy it and release it, "rescue" it from its "captivity."[39] When I bought the old pipe for the stem, I was told to bury it. It was only when I felt guided to smoke it at Devil's Lake that I felt compelled to retrieve the buried bowl and put it into service.

Loss of Power of a Pipe

What is happening when a pipe begins to lose its power? Anything that hampers the relationship between you and the pipe. The most important hindrance is your own intent. Its effectiveness will be hindered to the extent that those involved don't remain in fresh, ongoing communication with the pipe. You may be neglecting the pipe by not cleaning and caring for it properly or by going long periods of time without smoking it. You and your pipe may be drifting apart. Or improper handling and storage, public display, making the pipe subject to negative intent, close proximity with a woman on her moon, or alcohol or drug use can weaken the bond and the pipe's power.[40]

A psychotherapy client of mine once told me that he had been a pipe carrier for some time. But once when he lapsed and began doing drugs again, he actually smoked pot in his pipe. Afterwards he was very remorseful and felt that he didn't have a right to use the pipe, so he buried it. Many years later, he had maintained his sobriety for a very long time. He thought about taking up the pipe again, but it had been so long he had forgotten where he had buried it. Shortly after that he began digging to make himself a root cellar, and immediately he unearthed the pipe. When he was ready, the pipe appeared.

Unawakened display pipes may have stems and bowls permanently attached or the hole sealed in the bowl, so they may never be awakened.[41]

Exception: some elders say it's acceptable to have a pipe that has been "retired" through proper ceremony on a family altar or some other place of honor. Pipes are retired from service for many reasons—for example, because the bowl is developing a crack.[42]

Improper Use of Tobacco

Many people think of tobacco as a terrible thing, killing and enslaving millions. But the herb has beneficial properties as well. It protects other nearby plants against bug infestations and it has tremendous curative properties. For example, it can be used as an emetic and poultice.

Before European contact, tobacco was not used for purely pleasurable purposes but was strictly used as medicine—both in the physical and the spiritual realm. Today, like so many other things sacred, tobacco has been misused, causing destruction instead of its divinely intended purpose of healing and restoration. As with any medicine, to overindulge is to risk great harm from a beneficial agent.[43]

All of the additives in tobacco to enhance a nicotine addiction are the main killers, along with the poison in the paper to help it burn. The spirit of any plant can be compromised when it is used recreationally rather than in a sacred manner for ceremony or healing.

There is a great deal of difference on all levels between smoking tobacco recreationally and using tobacco as a sacred substance in ceremony. I have known many pipe carriers, non-Native and Native, who smoke tobacco recreationally—usually cigarettes. The intent and purpose of smoking a cigarette, cigar, or recreational pipe is to gain pleasure by feeding an addiction. There is no value beyond immediate oral pleasure, and the passive smoke that is "given away" to others in the vicinity isn't even helpful to them.

Commercial tobacco isn't pure, but is laced with hundreds of additives—including *more* nicotine—to insure a continued addiction. The paper encasing a cigarette is laced with strychnine to help it burn. And when having a cigarette, smokers inhale the smoke into their lungs. In a pipe ceremony, when sacred smoke is breathed in—after it briefly inter-acts inside the body of the smoker—it is immediately breathed out. The smoke isn't for the smoker but for the Great Spirit.

Unlike a pipe used for recreational smoking, the Sacred Pipe has been awakened, blessed, and bound to the pipe carrier, and when the bowl and stem are joined in ceremony, the pipe becomes a powerful tool to focus and channel the pipe carrier's intentions and prayers to the heavens. The Sacred Pipe is an earth-centered tool that helps join Earth, Heaven, and humankind in an interactional dynamic for the purpose of health and healing. The pipe carrier becomes a cocreator, and there is a directed connection with Spirit; and other spirits and beings join in during the ceremony as well.

In the pipe ceremony, smoke is a visible representation of prayers and intentions drifting heavenward. The intent of smoking is prayerful and its purpose is to give thanks to the Creator, to ask for health and help for humankind, and to bless, honor, and heal the Earth.

Historically, specific Native tribes became Tobacco Societies and took on the responsibility of growing and harvesting tobacco in a sacred manner for use in ceremony. In modern times, I have known many pipe carriers who grow their own tobacco plants, along with herbs for the smoking mixture. Or they pick the herbs in the wild. Most of the pipe carriers I have known gravitate toward the purer tobaccos. (Bull Durham is readily available and tends to be purer than other brands.) American Spirit tobacco company sells organic tobacco and some companies still produce organic herbal mixtures.

One may ask, "How can the spirit of a plant stay strong when it is used for recreational purposes and is destructive to one's health? Won't a sacred plant lose its power if it's used in a manner that has no sacred intent?" Well, peyote, which has been used in a sacred manner by indig-enous peoples for many years—but then became used recreationally—is still used in a sacred manner in the Native American (Peyote) Church. Church members certainly don't feel the plant has lost its potency.

Has tobacco? Probably not. Nothing I have read or been taught would suggest it has. Though tobacco can kill people, the herb itself isn't evil. Tobacco's divinely created properties are for the benefit of humankind. As a matter of fact, among one of the ancient tribes in the South Pacific where people commonly live to be one hundred or older, many tribesmen smoke organic tobacco they grow themselves.

But commercial tobacco that is mass produced, refined, and processed, with all its additives to insure a continued addiction, is in many ways a totally different substance from raw, natural organic tobacco, grown and smoked in a sacred manner. It's like comparing meat from an elk shot by a bow and arrow by a Native in the wild to a steer raised in captivity for commercial use, injected with antibiotics and hormones, and then unceremoniously slaughtered.

There are many reasons why the spirit of the tobacco plant probably hasn't been weakened through recreational use. First, tobacco wasn't used for recreational purposes until the European insurgence into the United States only a few hundred years ago—7,500 years *after* Natives began using tobacco in a sacramental manner. I believe the length of time Natives honored and used tobacco as a sacred substance helped it gather power and momentum early on. Using tobacco in a sacred manner with an attitude of reverence, honoring, and sincerity of intent, with a deep emotional connection to the plant enhances its power and keeps the life force of the plant strong. It's unlikely that a comparatively few years of abuse would have weakened the spirit of the plant.

I asked internationally-known herbalist Stephen Harrod Buhner, author of *Sacred Plant Medicine*[44] and many other medicine plant books, and he agreed in general with my assessment. However, he suggested I consult with his partner, Trishuwa, part-Cherokee and an herbalist who has presented at international herbal conferences, because she has had a special interest in tobacco in particular and studied it for a number of years. I must say I wasn't quite ready for her response. It was so powerful and heartfelt, I offer it as a gift in its entirety.

Tobacco is found in innumerable forms today and some propose that its spirit has been weakened. I disagree. Tobacco's spirit remains intact and strong. Albeit contained in a designer cigarette, seasoned with mint, diluted with preservatives and inbred for optimal crop production, its spirit still lives strong and vibrant. When smoked, whether it is conscious or an unconscious act, tobacco gives its gifts. The recreational smoker often taps into a quiet place, the place of timelessness where linear time seems less important, less demanding. And yes, this is part of the addiction, but it is also part of tobacco's power. For me, tobacco is the communicator and has the power to transmit our deepest concerns, genuine feelings that reside in our hearts.

Ah yes, we are challenged to pray consciously with such a great power, but when we do, we form a relationship with tobacco crafted with a willingness to love and know this sacred herb. Nevertheless smoked, chewed, snuffed whether heartfelt, genuine need is something we are aware of or not, I believe tobacco still carries that genuine message. It is its nature, its sacred destiny.

Clearly Trishuwa sees tobacco as so powerful that it can survive anything anyone does to it. The spirit of the tobacco plant still radiates through. And its power affects recreational smokers, whether they are aware of it or not. Maybe that's why smokers can take a long drag on a stimulant and slump back in a relaxed posture. Perhaps that peacefulness is more than feeding an addiction; it is subconsciously connecting with the spirit of tobacco.

Trishuwa goes on to say:

Although I romanticize my ancestors and their sacred relationship with tobacco, I don't know how it really was. I don't know how it would have been generations ago participating in ceremony with my community, my elders, and contemporaries who had always believed in the spirit and the power of tobacco as far back as they could remember. I do know their knowledge would have been part of my life, a foundation for my relationship with tobacco. Without the passing down of ancestral knowledge, we have a crisis of faith and most have forgotten how to talk to tobacco as an embodied spiritual being. The challenge of this time on sweet Mother Earth is to re-establish that faith, to continue to speak to tobacco although it may be adorned in the trappings of our times, to entwine our spirit with tobacco and respectfully ask for its help, its genuine participation in our life.[45]

And I believe that it is the particular responsibility of pipe carriers to connect with the spirit of tobacco as part of their special service to the planet and humankind.

* * *

Jim Tree points out that once you take up a pipe, you enter into a wonderful and demanding relationship, which can lead you to the highest expression of yourself. The Great Spirit has created the interdependence of all things. So with a new pipe, we need its direction and intervention; it needs us to care for it and provide the ceremonies through which it does its work.[46] And today more than ever before, the Earth needs healing, and we need a vehicle to help us keep up with the Earth changes during the most important spiritual transition in modern history.

* * *

The sun is now higher in the sky, its warmth spiriting away the morning chill. The sky is a clear, deep blue. The ancient whispers, the spirits of Devil's Lake—called Spirit Lake by the Native Americans who once lived on its shores—subside and lapse comfortably into silence. I smoke the last of the smoking mixture.

Holding the pipe at waist level, palms upward, I end the ceremony with a song:

Fly like an eagle,
Flying so high,
Circling the Universe,
On wings of pure Light.
Oh witchi tai tai
Witchi tai hai-o
Oh witchi tai tai
Witchi tai hai-o
Fly like an eagle,
Flying so high,
Circling the Universe,
On wings of pure Love.

After raising the Sacred Pipe above my head, I say:

I thank You Creator,
for the privilege of smoking this pipe
and I say, yes, yes, yes, to your divine will.

I disconnect the pipe, clean it, wrap the bowl and stem separately, and return it to the sacred bundle. Like the Native Americans for hundreds, if not thousands, of years before, I realize that it is through finding the God within and our place in God's web of creation that we might, through the Sacred Pipe, strive to heal ourselves, all our relations, and Mother Earth. Through the Sacred Pipe, there may be hope for us and our children.

Notes

INTRODUCTION

1. Jordan Paper, *Offering Smoke: The Sacred Pipe and Native American Religion* (Moscow, Idaho: University of Idaho Press, 1988), 8.
2. The Good Red Road is the sacred path of conducting oneself in a way that puts us in peace and harmony with all living things.
3. Jim Tree, *The Way of the Sacred Pipe* (Hamilton, MT: Blue Sky, 2004), 9. I am indebted to Jim Tree for his contribution to the understanding of the Sacred Pipe. Two-thirds of his book includes interesting and inspirational stories (many of them, his personal experiences) that convey a deep respect and appreciation for Native spirituality and the Sacred Pipe. The last third of the book involves specific instructions about the care and use of the pipe. Though I was well aware of many of his ideas, when one of them jogged my memory or reminded me of something I wanted to include, I cited the page number from his work.
4. Ed McGaa (Eagle Man), *Rainbow Tribe: Ordinary People Journeying on the Red Road* (San Francisco: Harper, 1992), 254–55.
5. Ibid.; the whole book covers the idea.
6. Jay Cleve, "Way of the Sacred Pipe," *Gnosis: Journal of Inner Western Traditions* 47 (Spring 1998): 25–28.
7. Paper, *Offering Smoke.*
8. Tree, *Way of the Sacred Pipe,* 1–105.
9. Ibid., 13.
10. Ibid., 14.
11. Ibid.
12. Robert B. Pickering, *Seeing the White Buffalo* (Boulder, CO: Denver Museum of Natural History Press, 1997), 144.
13. http://heyokamagazine.com/heyoka.6.LBW.1.htm.
14. Paper, *Offering Smoke*, 2.
15. Pickering, *Seeing the White Buffalo*, 19.

16. Ibid., 55.
17. Ibid., 1.
18. "Miracle's Second Chance," Snow Owl 9/10/06, http://snowwowl.com/contents.html. With the death of Snow Owl, the site was taken over, cut back, and summarized. Unfortunately, some information was lost.
19. Pickering, *Seeing the White Buffalo*, 12–13.
20. Ibid., 71.
21. Nicolya Christi, *2012: A Clarion Call* (Rochester, VT: Bear and Company, 2011), 60–61.
22. Pickering, *Seeing the White Buffalo*, 8.
23. Ibid., 131.
24. "Miracle's Second Chance," Snow Owl 9/10/06, http://snowwowl.com/contents.html.
25. "Special Edition—Update on Miracle's Second Chance," 12/6/06, http://snowwowl.com/contents.html.
26. Ibid.
27. Ibid.
28. Pickering, *Seeing the White* Buffalo, 56–57.
29. Christi, *Clarion Call*, 2.
30. Pickering, *Seeing the White Buffalo*, 65, 139.
31. Frank Waters, *Book of the Hopi* (New York: Penguin, 1977).
32. Sun Bear and Wabun Wind, *Black Dawn/Bright Day: Indian Prophecies for the Millennium That Reveal the Fate of the Earth* (New York: Fireside, 1992).
33. Tom Brown, Jr., *The Quest: One Man's Search for Peace, Insight, and Healing in an Endangered World* (New York: Berkley, 2000).
34. Geoff Stray, *Beyond 2012: Catastrophe or Awakening?* (Rochester, VT: Bear and Company, 2009), 9–56.
35. Christi, *Clarion Call*, 2.
36. Globalstationary Operational Environmental Satellites: http://www.oso.noaa.gov/goes.
37. Jim Oschman and Nora Oschman, "Science Measures the Human Energy Field," p. 1, http://www.reiki.org/reikinews/ScienceMeasures.htm; Rollin McCraty, PhD, Raymond Trevor Bradley, PhD, and Dana Tomasino, BA, "The Heart Has Its Own 'Brain' Consciousness," p. 1, http://www.mindmscleblog.com/heart-has-its-own-consciousness; "The Heart is an Electromagnetic

Field," p. 1, http.distantenergyhealing.blogspot.com/2009/12/heart-is-electromagnetic-field.html.

38. "The Heart has an Electromagnetic Field," p. 1; Mary Ann Reynolds, "The Heart's Energy Field," Jan. 11, 2012, p. 2, http://wellbodymindspirit.com/2012/01/11the-heart's-energy-field.

39. HeartMath, http//:www.heartmath.org; Global Coherence Initiative: Community Building, Environmental Responsibility, Heart Coherence Plan, http://www.glcoherence.org/about-us/about.html.

Chapter 1

THE SACRED PIPE

1. Paper, *Offering Smoke*, 43–50 (see intro., n. 1).

2. Evelyn Eaton, *Snowy Earth Comes Gliding* (Independence, CA: Draco Foundation, 1974), 99.

3. Robert A. Murray, *Pipes on the Plains* (Pipestone, MN: Pipestone Indian Shrine Association, 1968), 22.

4. Paper, *Offering Smoke*, 66.

5. Ibid., 53.

6. John G. Neihardt, *Black Elk Speaks* (New York: Washington Square Press, 1972), 3.

7. Joseph Epes Brown, *The Sacred Pipe* (New York: Penguin, 1971), 3.

8. William Stolzman, *The Pipe and Christ* (Chamberlain, SD: Tipi Press, 1986).

9. Tree, *Way of the Sacred Pipe*, 44 (see intro., n. 3).

10. Sun Bear, Bear Tribe Medicine Society Apprenticeship Program (Spokane, WA: Vision Mountain, 1988).

11. Paper, *Offering Smoke*, 5.

12. Ibid., 12.

13. Ibid., 13.

14. Louis Seig, *Tobacco, Peace Pipes, and Indians* (Palmer Lake, CO: Filter Press, 1971).

15. Michael F. Steltenkamp, *The Sacred Vision: Native American Religion and Its Practice Today* (Mahwah, NJ: Paulist Press, 1982), 25.

16. Paper, *Offering Smoke*, 21.

17. Ibid., 25.

18. Hartley Burr Alexander, *The World's Rim* (Lincoln, NE: University of Nebraska, 1967), 3.
19. Murray, *Pipes on the Plains*, 16–17.
20. Stolzman, *The Pipe and Christ*, 169–72.
21. Ibid., 67–74.
22. Thomas E. Mails, *Fools Crow* (Lincoln, NE: University of Nebraska Press, 1979).
23. Arval Looking Horse, "The Sacred Pipe in Modern Life," in Raymond DeMallie, and Douglas Parks, eds., *Sioux Indian Religion* (Norman, OK: University of Oklahoma, 1987), 69.
24. Paul B. Steinmetz, "The Sacred Pipe in American Indian Religion," *American Indian Culture and Research Journal* 8, no. 3 (1984): 27.
25. Steltenkamp, *Sacred Vision*, 25.
26. Tree, *Way of the Sacred Pipe*, 44.
27. Murray, *Pipes on the Plains*, 19.
28. George Catlin, *Letters and Notes on the North American Indians* (New York: Gramercy Books, 1977), 325.
29. Ibid., 326.
30. Ibid., 322.
31. Murray, *Pipes on the Plains*, 11.
32. Ibid., 51.
33. Jim PathFinder Ewing, "Does Looking Back Woman Have 'The' Sacred Pipe?" pp. 1–7, www.Lookingbackwoman.ca/bluskywaters.htm.
34. Murray, *Pipes on the* Plains, 6–12.
35. Paper, *Offering Smoke*, 24.
36. Seig, *Tobacco, Peace Pipes, and Indians*, 14.
37. Tree, *Way of the Sacred Pipe*, 44.
38. Ibid., 45.
39. Ibid.
40. Ibid., 46.
41. Paper, *Offering Smoke*, 53.
42. Seig, *Tobacco, Peace Pipes, and Indians*, 1–9.
43. Murray, *Pipes on the Plains*, 13.
44. Tree, *Way of the Sacred Pipe*, 96.

45. Murray, *Pipes on the Plains*, 13.
46. Paper, *Offering Smoke*, 98.
47. Tree, *Way of the Sacred Pipe*, 50.
48. Ibid., 68.
49. Ibid., 62.
50. Ibid., 73.

Chapter 2

THE MEDICINE WHEEL

1. J. E. Brown, *Sacred Pipe* (see chap. 1, n. 7).
2. John Redtail Freesoul, *Breath of the Invisible* (Wheaton, IL: Quest Books, 1993), 48.
3. Ibid., 47, 48, 54.
4. Sun Bear, Wabun Wind, and Crysalis Mulligan, *Dancing with the Wheel* (New York: Touchstone, 1991), 1.
5. Roy I. Wilson, *Medicine Wheels* (New York: Crossroad, 1994), 9.
6. Freesoul, *Breath of the Invisible*, 49.
7. Sun Bear, *Dancing with the Wheel*, xvi.
8. Mary E. Loomis, *Dancing the Wheel of Psychological Types* (Wilmette, IL: Chiron, 1991), 1.
9. Ibid.
10. Hyemeyohsts Storm, *Seven Arrows* (New York: Ballantine, 1972), 4.
11. Loomis, *Dancing the Wheel*, 1.
12. Ibid., x.
13. Ibid., 2.
14. Ibid., 4.
15. Ibid., 5.
16. Unless otherwise specified, the building and description of the Medicine Wheel is from Sun Bear's vision as described in his book *Dancing with the Wheel* (see note 4 for this chapter), and the teachings I received from Sun Bear and Wabun in the apprenticeship program and Medicine Wheel Gatherings in the late 1980s and 1990s.
17. Loren Cruden, *Compass of the Heart* (Rochester, VT: 1996), 196.
18. Joseph Epes Brown, *Animals of the Soul* (Rockport, MA: Element, 1992), 187.

19. The following books have been cited multiple times in the "Spirit Keepers of the Four Directions" section of the "Medicine Wheel" chapter. Specific pages have been cited: (a) Ted Andrews, *Animal-Speak: The Spiritual and Magical Powers of Creatures Great and Small* (St. Paul, MN: Llewellyn, 1996), eagle: 136–141; coyote: 260–62; bear: 250–52; buffalo: 254–55; hawk: 152–55; wolf: 323–25; cougar: 259–60. (b) Stephen Harrod Buhner, *Sacred Plant Medicine* (Rochester, VT: Bear and Company, 2006), 130. (c) D. J. Conway, *Animal Magick*, (St. Paul, MN: Llewellyn, 1995), eagle: 162–64; coyote: 89; bear: 104–6; buffalo: 107–8; hawk: 168–69; wolf: 93–96; cougar: 76. (d) Dolfyn and Swimming Wolf, *Shamanic Wisdom II* (Oakland, CA: Earthspirit, 1994), eagle: 52–54; coyote: 40–43; bear: 23–25; buffalo: 29–31; hawk: 66–68; wolf: 29–31. (e) Jessica Dawn Palmer, *Animal Wisdom: The Definitive Guide to the Myth, Folklore and Medicine Power of Animals* (London: Thorsons, 2001), eagle: 135–44; coyote: 81–86; bear: 31–41; buffalo: 55–63; hawk: 189–94; wolf: 366–77; cougar: 76–81. (f) Jamie Sams and David Carson, *Medicine Cards: The Discovery of Power through the Ways of Animals* (Santa Fe, NM: Bear and Company, 1988), eagle: 41–45; coyote: 85–89; bear: 57–61; buffalo: 113–117; hawk: 45–46; wolf: 97–101.

20. J. E. Brown, *Animals of the Soul*, 4.

21. Sun Bear's *Dancing with the Wheel* (see note 4 for this chapter) is used exclusively for the "Powers of the Four Cardinal Directions" section.

22. Freesoul, *Breath of the Invisible*, 86.

Chapter 3
CEREMONIES WITH THE SACRED PIPE

1. Sun Bear, *Dancing with the Wheel*, 9–10 (see chap. 2, n. 4).

2. Ibid., 10.

3. Joseph Epes Brown, *The Spiritual Legacy of the American Indian* (New York: Crossroads, 1982), 101.

4. Ibid., 103.

5. Hans Wilhelm Leo, "Sweating the Body, Sweating the Soul: A Cross-Cultural Experience," *Wildfire* 4, no. 3: 25.

6. Joseph Epes Brown, *The Sacred Pipe: Black Elk's Account of the Seven Rites of the Oglala Sioux* (Norman, OK: University of Oklahoma, 1953), 32.

7. McGaa, *Rainbow Tribe*, 67 (see intro., n. 4).

8. Cruden, *Compass of the Heart*, 170–171 (see chap. 2, n. 17).

9. Joseph Bruchac, *The Native American Sweat Lodge* (Freedom, CA: Crossing, 1993), 45.

10. Freesoul, *Breath of the Invisible*, 28–29 (see chap. 2, n. 2).

11. Ed McGaa, *Mother Earth Spirituality* (San Francisco, CA: Harper, 1990), 67.

12. J. E. Brown, *Sacred Pipe*, 32, 44.

13. Brad Steiger, *Indian Medicine Power* (Gloucester, PA: Para Research, 1984), 36.

14. Cruden, *Compass of the Heart*, 196.

15. Ibid., 105.

16. McGaa, *Rainbow Tribe*, 103.

17. Freesoul, *Breath of the Invisible*, 41.

18. Cruden, *Compass of the Heart*, 194.

19. Ibid., 196.

20. The Q'ero are the last of the Incas who fled to the high Andes mountains during the Spanish Conquest. Many of the elders didn't come down from the mountains until very recent years.

21. Freesoul, *Breath of the Invisible*, 34–35.

22. J. E. Brown, *Spiritual Legacy*, 101.

23. _____, *Sacred Pipe*, 32, 44.

24. Steiger, *Indian Medicine Power*, 36.

25. J. E. Brown, *Spiritual Legacy*, 103–4.

26. Ibid.,104.

27, McGaa, *Mother Earth Spirituality*, 85–89.

28. J. E. Brown, *Spiritual Legacy*, 105.

Chapter 4

NATIVE AMERICAN SPIRITUAL PHILOSOPHY

1. Tom Brown, Jr., *The Vision* (New York: Berkley, 1988), 3.

2. Cruden, *Compass of the Heart*, 2 (see chap. 2, n. 17).

3. Freesoul, *Breath of the Invisible*, 85 (see chap. 2, n. 2).

4. J. E. Brown, *Spiritual Legacy* (see chap. 3, n. 3). Since this book is exceptional in its presentation of Native spiritual philosophy, I have drawn heavily

from it in both the cosmology and theology sections. Except where someone else is cited, the ideas come from Brown. I have tried to reduce some of his wording, though it is very poetic, in order to be more economical—without, I hope, losing the essence of his profound ideas.

5. McGaa, *Rainbow Tribe* (see intro., n. 4).

6. T. Brown, *Vision*, 108.

7. J. E. Brown, *Sacred Pipe*, 3 (see chap. 1, n. 7).

8. Ron Zeilinger, *Sacred Ground: Reflections on Lakota Spirituality and the Gospel* (Chamberlain, SD: Tipi Press, 1986), 102.

9. Ananda Coomaraswamy, *Hinduism and Buddhism* (Westport, CT: Greenwood Press, 1971), 6.

10. Dennis Tedlock, *Handbook of North American Indians* 1, chap. 50, William C. Sturtevant, ed. (Washington, DC: Smithsonian Institute). Found in J. E. Brown's *Legacy*, p. 4. Brown cited it before it was published (no date).

11. Arnold Toynbee, *New York Times*, September 16, 1973.

12. Tree, *Way of the Sacred Pipe*, 36–37 (see intro., n. 3).

13. Zeilinger, *Sacred Ground*, 102.

14. Freesoul, *Breath of the Invisible*, 12.

15. Paper, *Offering Smoke*, 38 (see intro., n. 1).

16. Ibid., 39.

17. Vinson Brown, *Voices of Earth and Sky* (Happy Camp, CA: Naturegraph, 1976), 117.

18. Ibid.

19. Spoken to a group I was with in Joy Lake, Nevada, in 1988. At the time, I had the privilege of having some long talks with Bill Lyon, who was finishing his research for the book he then soon published: William S. Lyon, *Black Elk: The Sacred Ways of a Lakota* (San Francisco, CA: HarperCollins, 1990). The almost exact quote appears on page 40.

20. Eaton, *Snowy Earth*, 102 (see chap. 1, n. 2).

21. Paper, *Offering Smoke*, 56.

22. V. Brown, *Voices of Earth and Sky*, 118.

23. Ibid., 106.

24. Ibid.

25. Eaton, *Snowy Earth*, 103.

26. Freesoul, *Breath of the Invisible*, 14.

27. Ibid., 13.
28. Ibid., 140.
29. Ibid., 12.
30. J. E. Brown, *Sacred Pipe*, 45.
31. Ibid., 115.

Chapter 5
SMOKING THE SACRED PIPE
 1. Paper, *Offering Smoke*, 61 (see intro., n. 1).
 2. Ibid., 57.
 3. John (Fire) Lame Deer and Richard Erdoes, *Lame Deer, Seeker of Visions* (New York: Touchstone, 1972), 12.
 4. Tree, *Way of the Sacred Pipe*, 16 (see intro., n. 3). Note: I have drawn heavily from Jim Tree's book. I received my most intensive training on the pipe in the late 1980s and early 1990s, and Tree's book refreshed my memory on the specific care and maintenance of the pipe. Though some of it wasn't new information for me, I want to credit him whenever he offers useful information.
 5. Ibid., 16.
 6. Ibid., 58.
 7. Pickering, *Seeing the White Buffalo*, 18 (see intro., n. 12).
 8. Freesoul, *Breath of the Invisible*, 12–13 (see chap. 2, n. 2).
 9. J. E. Brown, *Spiritual Legacy*, 45 (see chap. 3, n. 3).
10. Lame Deer, *Seeker of Visions*, 252–53.
11. Ben Black Bear, Jr., "Cannupa—The Sacred Pipe: The Basis of Lakota Spirituality": http://www.bluecloud.org/2.html.
12. J. E. Brown, *Spiritual Legacy*, 51.
13. Eaton, *Snowy Earth*, 101 (see chap. 1, n. 2).
14. Buhner, *Sacred Plant Medicine*, 109 (see chap. 2, n. 19b).
15. Ibid., 110.
16. Tree, *Way of the Sacred Pipe*, 14, 16.
17. Ibid., 49–50.
18. Ibid., 17.
19. Ibid., 104.
20. Ibid., 64.

21. Ibid., 72.
22. Ibid., 78.
23. Buhner, *Sacred Plant*, 105.
24. Ibid.
25. Ibid., 112.
26. Tree, *Way of the Sacred Pipe*, 64.
27. Ibid., 68.
28. Ibid., 72.
29. Ibid., 77.
30. Buhner, *Sacred Plant*, 114.
31. Tree, *Way of the Sacred Pipe*, 85.
32. Ibid., 83.
33. Ibid.
34. Ibid., 84.
35. Ibid., 7, 9.
36. Ibid., 55, 65.
37. Ibid., 95.
38. Ibid., 55.
39. Ibid.
40. Ibid., 93–95.
41. Ibid., 56.
42. Ibid., 55.
43. Ibid., 96.
44. Stephen Buhner has been studying plants for many years, has written many excellent books on plant medicine, and is a widely recognized herbalist.
45. Trishuwa is Stephen Buhner's partner; he asked her to contact me since her focus has been primarily on tobacco for several years. She is a founding member of the Foundation for Gaian Studies and has spoken at international symposiums on herbal medicine and a variety of Native spiritual traditions.
46. Tree, *Way of the Sacred Pipe*, 49.

Index

Index

Index

Quest Books

encourages open-minded inquiry into
world religions, philosophy, science, and the arts
in order to understand the wisdom of the ages,
respect the unity of all life, and help people explore
individual spiritual self-transformation.

Its publications are generously supported by
The Kern Foundation,
a trust committed to Theosophical education.

Quest Books is the imprint of
the Theosophical Publishing House,
a division of the Theosophical Society in America.
For information about programs, literature,
on-line study, membership benefits, and international centers,
see www.theosophical.org
or call 800-669-1571 or (outside the U.S.) 630-668-1571.

Related Quest Titles

*Manual for the Peacemaker: An Iroquois Legend
to Heal Self and Society,* by Jean Houston

Native Healer, by Medicine Grizzlybear Lake

The Shaman and the Medicine Wheel, by Evelyn Eaton

*The Vision Keepers: Walking for Native Americans
and the Earth,* by Doug Alderson

To order books or a complete Quest catalog,
call 800-669-9425 or (outside the U.S.) 630-665-0130.